THE NEWEST LONDON SPY

MULLER

THE NEWEST LONDON SPY

edited by Tim Heald

Cartoons by Colin Wheeler

FREDERICK MULLER

London Melbourne Auckland Johannesburg

© Frederick Muller 1988
© introduction and his own contribution Tim Heald 1988
© cartoons Colin Wheeler 1988

Permission is gratefully acknowledged to quote an extract from
Collected Poems, John Betjeman, John Murray (Publishers) Ltd

First published in 1988 by Frederick Muller
an imprint of Century Hutchinson Ltd
Brookmount House, 62–65 Chandos Place, London WC2N 4NW

Century Hutchinson Publishing Group (Australia) Pty Ltd
PO Box 496, 16–22 Church Street, Hawthorn, Melbourne,
Victoria 3122

Century Hutchinson Group (NZ) Ltd
PO Box 40-086, 32–34 View Road, Glenfield, Auckland 10

Century Hutchinson (SA) Pty Ltd
PO Box 337, Bergvlei 2012, South Africa

Set in Linotron Sabon by
Rowland Phototypesetting Ltd
Bury St Edmunds, Suffolk
Printed and bound in Great Britain by
Anchor Brendon Ltd, Tiptree, Essex

British Library Cataloguing in Publication Data
The newest London spy.
  1. London (England) – Description – 1981–
  I. Heald, Tim
  914.21′04858   DA684.2

ISBN 0-09-173658-7

CONTENTS

CONTRIBUTORS

Alexandra Artley, David Benedictus, Marcel Berlins, Anthony Blond, Simon Brett, Euan Cameron, Roger Clarke, Stephen Cook, Hunter Davies, W. F. Deedes, Siobhan Dowd, Gavin Ewart, Dennis Farr, William Foster, Alexander Frater, Alexander and Emma Heald, Mel Henry, Rosemary Hill, Philip Howard, Francis King, Ann Leslie, Karen Leslie, Willy Loyd, J. G. Links, Richard Mabey, Timothy Matthews, Hugh Montgomery-Massingberd, Genevieve Muinzer, Ken Powell, Roger Protz, Josephine Pullein-Thompson, John Rae, Timothy Satchell, Richard Simon, Clive Sinclair, Gavin Stamp, Danusia Stok, Ion Trewin, Julia Tugendhat, Marina Vaizey, Christopher Warman, Annasue McCleave Wilson, Tom Vaughan, Hugo Vickers, Betka Zamoyska.

FOREWORD

Ned Ward, a London publican, wrote the first alternative guide to London in 1703. Westminster Abbey and Covent Garden were there, though described with a more than usually astringent eye. So were tarts and taverns. Ward baited the inmates at Bedlam and watched a woman being whipped at Bridewell. London as observed by Ward seemed dangerously louche and perversely exciting. It was the year Isaac Newton became President of the Royal Society and the year in which the English first began to drink port.

The 1960s, popularly characterised as the 'Swinging Sixties', were also, for London, years of fast living, hedonism and sensuality. In 1966 Hunter Davies, then 'Atticus' of the *Sunday Times*, put together an update of Ward's *Spy*. The sixties' book ranged from statues to lesbians, warned that it would cost two people £10 for an evening out in a nightclub, and claimed that if you walked along Oxford Street during the rush hour, you would always see at least three people topple over and fall down.

Reading through that volume today the world of the sixties seems almost as distant as the world of 1703. The telephone numbers for instance: GERard and FLAxman, JUNiper and TERminus, MUSeum and PRImrose. All gone along with one-pound notes and threepenny bits and farthings. In those heady times there was a young man called David Bailey on PRI 9955 who would, according to the *New London Spy* take a 'modern' photograph 'showing your hairy armpits' for a hundred guineas! Whatever happened to guineas?

Twenty years in the Almighty's sight is not even an evening gone, but it has been time enough to remove any number of landmarks and institutions. In those days Max Aitken and

Uffa Fox were virtually synonymous with the Daily Express Boat Show and Randolph Churchill with White's Club. Many of this book's readers won't even have heard of them.

Sexual mores have changed beyond recognition. The 1966 *Spy* advised readers on no account to spend a night in a London hotel with a person of the opposite sex to whom they were not married. 'It will turn out a bleak and jumpy experience.' You might get away with it in a suite but hotels, apparently, did not like being used as brothels. Nowadays hoteliers may still harbour such objections but they are seldom voiced. In the sixties people in search of easy, foolproof divorces still went to hotels with 'stooges' (fee £75–100) who could be identified in court when you sought to prove adultery. As far as homosexuality was concerned, 'We are as a nation only moving slowly towards the recognition that homosexual relationships between consenting adults are not criminal acts.'

Among hotels the brand leaders have survived largely unchanged save for the Berkeley which moved from Mayfair to Belgravia. Soho was still *the* restaurant area. The Coq d'Or had not yet become Langan's Brasserie. Mme Prunier was still operating in St James' and Nick's Diner in Fulham. The writer on Indian London said Indian food in the capital was second-rate and recommended the Kwality in Whitfield Street with the words, 'Their speciality is tandori chicken and if you think you have tried every possible way of cooking chicken, then a great surprise awaits you.' Nowadays, of course, there are more 'Tandori' restaurants than 'Indian'. Nouvelle Cuisine was unheard of and Covent Garden was still a vegeable market, not a tourist trap.

Real Ale had not arrived. Nor had the pub with the 'theme'. The 1966 *Spy* index had no entry under 'wine bar' and no mention of McDonalds' hamburgers. When people talked about 'franchise', they meant the right to vote. It took a Pan-Am pilot called Jim Zockoll to change that with a franchised drain-clearance service called Dyno-Rod. He used those new-fangled advertisement boards on the tube and yellow pages, too. No mention of those in the sixties. And in those days, of course, smoking was still sexy, virile and allowed everywhere.

Abortion was still 'absolutely illegal'. Blades was still 'a young man's tailor' and would knock you up a suit for seventy guineas. Those guineas again! For just one you could catch a day-return steamer to Southend. For two you could take a barrel organ with you on the cruise. The only cricket nets in winter were at Alf Gover's in Clapham. Don Wilson's reign at the new indoor school at Lord's was hardly even a gleam in the eye. The Bath Club still existed. So did the United Services. The Groucho didn't. And the final conclusion at the end of the final sixties' chapter was that when a foreign chappie arrived in London he had arrived at 'the heart of the most civilised human community in the world.' That's another lost aspect of London: self-confidence. Or is it arrogance?

When Anthony Blond, who had published Hunter Davies' 1966 book, proposed a new *New London Spy* the first thing to be queried was the title. *Spy* was originally the Chinese word for a crack or crevice – (no, not chink) – and in the purest sense it simply meant anyone who looked through a crack in the wall or a tear in the curtain to observe what others did not wish observed. Latterly however any book with *Spy* in the title is assumed to be a work of fiction featuring the CIA or the KGB. There have been espionage novels since Fenimore Cooper wrote *The Spy* in 1821 but in the sixties spy novels became so successful that to use the word in any other sense than the one employed by Deighton, Le Carré and others was positively misleading. Nevertheless this book is in a direct line of descent from the 1703 *Spy* and the sixties' *Spy* so we decided to keep the word in the title at the risk of confusing thriller readers. It's become a tradition.

Like its predecessor this newest *Spy* does not pretend to be comprehensive. It is deliberately and necessarily selective and opinionated. On the grounds that no one person could possibly have the expertise to write with authority on so many

diverse subjects it has been written by a great many different hands. Last time there were just over thirty. This time there are about half as many again.

In 1966 the *Spy* said it would be devoted to 'pleasures which haven't been charted before – from sex to sermons.' In fact it included quite a lot of pain along with the pleasure. A section on 'Successful Sickness' ('Find yourself an expensive Harley Street quack without delay', for instance), and a whole chapter on being 'Down and Out'. This book is also prejudiced in favour of fun but not exclusively so.

Writing about things 'which haven't been charted before' is more difficult today. In the sixties the typical guidebook was staid and bland; nowadays such books tend to be much racier and to deal with what used to be taboo – sex in all its forms, drugs, crime, gambling. Hunter Davies has produced another London guide of his own with such entries as 'Boring Hotels' and 'Sex and Friends'. So has another of the *Spy*'s sixties' contributors, David Benedictus, who is, if anything, even more relentlessly chirpy and eclectic. He gives awards to London's 'Best Post Office' (Lisson Grove) and 'Best Horse Trough' (Richmond Gate). When the last *Spy* appeared, there was no such thing as *Time Out*. There was no English edition of *Michelin*, no *Good Hotel Guide* and Raymond Postgate still had three years to go as editor of the *Good Food Guide*. For those who want crisp, up-to-the-minute information on every conceivable subject London is now incomparably better served than twenty years ago.

John Buchan, defending the talking of 'shop', once said that the most riveting thing in the world was to hear an expert on his own subject. The guiding principle of this book has been that the writers should be writing as insiders letting in a little light on some part of London which is particularly theirs. It may be where they live or where they work; the ethnic or religious group to which they belong; or even the vice to which they are most prone. But they all write as insiders. Even, to take the most extreme example, the section on London's prisons, is contributed by someone who has spent years inside them.

In the sixties a list of contributors was printed at the front of the book but no names were attached to individual articles. I have followed that formula again. It means you can have an entertaining time trying to work out who wrote what and it also means that the editor feels he has a freer than usual hand to interfere with style, opinions or even facts! Some of the pieces in the book are the work of many hands. I asked contributors to avoid the first person but not everyone did. It would have been possible to edit the 'I's' out altogether but on one or two occasions it would have meant losing a particular anecdote or an extra little bit of authority and so I have kept them in. I hope this doesn't bring readers up with a terrible jolt. I think the inconsistency is allowable in a book which is almost as much of an anthology as a guide.

This *Spy* is intended to be useful but it is deliberately intended to be less useful than others. In fact it would be best considered as a companion. One of the reasons that so many modern guides are in paperback or even magazine form is that a certain sort of information dates impossibly fast. If you want phone numbers, you had best go to the phone book; if you want to know the time of the Changing of the Guard, call Daily Telegraph Information or the London Tourist Board or even the Palace itself. Or invest in another sort of guide. The point about this guide is that it attempts to get beneath the city's skin and to portray it through the eyes of Londoners themselves. Like Ned Ward's and Hunter Davies' *Spy*s it is much, though not exclusively, concerned with pleasure. It is also, just as much, concerned with people and places – which is how I have arranged it. The arrangement works but is not an absolute. There are people in 'Places', places framing the 'People' and a little pleasure everywhere. By reading judiciously you should be able to extract a lot of enjoyment from London, but even if you never come to London you should be able to get almost as much enjoyment just from reading it.

Tim Heald

PLACES

LOST PROPERTIES

If Rome is the Eternal City, London is the transitory city, a place of senseless, sometimes unintelligible, change and growth. Victorian London was the imperial city, a world phenomenon. Late twentieth-century London, for all its delights, has an air of melancholy. So many of its glories have departed. The faceless mediocrity of Victoria Street is a symbol of all that is worst in modern London.

Hitler's bombs wounded London severely, but the damage could have been made good. Instead, after a decade or more of inertia, the planners and developers embarked on a new blitz. The rebuilt City is a good place to study this rush to destruction. The greater part of the fabric which survived in 1945 has gone since then: banks and insurance offices, pubs and restaurants, the old Stock Exchange and Coal Exchange (a wondrous domed structure, pulled down in 1962 for road widening), stations like Blackfriars and Broad Street (replaced by office blocks) and the Lloyds Building, once a noble classical palazzo by Sir Edwin Cooper, now a fading novelty by Richard Rogers. The only hope for what is left is that the developers can be persuaded to pull down some of the banalities of the last quarter-century, rather than the surviving historic fragments.

East of the City, the Luftwaffe had done its best to flatten Cockney London but it was left to the 1960s and 1970s to destroy the riverside quays and warehouses, to rebuild St Katharine's Dock as a tawdry sub-Disneyland and to flatten the noble 'stacks' of Daniel Alexander's London Docks to make way for . . . Fortress Wapping. Cutler Street, the magnificent warehouse complex on the edge of Spitalfields, was mostly demolished in 1978–9 for office development.

Euston Station, with its sublime 'arch', is the most famous

'. . . planners and developers embarked on a new blitz.'

casualty of all, replaced by the soulless new 'gateway to the north'. All was destroyed in 1962–3, after the matter had been debated (and approved) by Harold Macmillan's Cabinet. St Pancras might easily have followed. The mood was ruthless, and there were plans even to rebuild the whole of Whitehall. London University destroyed the Imperial Institute in South Kensington (though it had to preserve the tower, a pathetic remnant) and went on to wreck Bloomsbury. (Woburn Square, one of the most attractive in the area, succumbed in 1970.)

The destroyers were to be found everywhere. The Church of England pulled down most of Wren's Christ Church, Newgate Street, as late as 1974. Victorian churches were little valued, though the spires of St Saviour's, Warwick Avenue, and Holy Trinity, Paddington, were landmarks amidst faded stucco streets. Both were toppled, along with fifty more steeples, spires and porticoes. The government let Woolwich Arsenal rot and then cleared away the buildings which had oiled the British war machine. Big stores, like Gamage's and the Army & Navy, found a new image in banal box-like buildings.

The Victorians injected fantasy into everyday life, so that Fitzroy Doll's Imperial Hotel in Russell Square threw together the styles of many nations and centuries without regard for propriety. The result was memorable – indeed, unforgettable. It was torn down in 1966 and a new hotel, a tawdry creation in concrete and flashy finishes, was thrown up for the tourists. Two years later, the demolition men moved into Alfred Waterhouse's St Paul's School at Hammersmith, clearing away a masterpiece in red brick and terracotta. Knightsbridge Barracks went for a new concrete fortress – the march of concrete seemed irresistible. Birkbeck's Bank on High Holborn, with its gorgeous, tile-clad rotunda, a banker's version of the British Museum Reading Room, was another sixties' casualty. The destroyers took away the fantasy and the glamour and created mediocrity and vulgarity – not even the disapproval of Buckingham Palace could stop the Hilton

Hotel being built on Park Lane (on the site of Londonderry House, one of the few private palaces to survive the carnage of the inter-war years). Yet the architects of the 1930s created a glamorous new architecture, seen in the super-cinemas of the suburbs – now fast dwindling – and the factories of the Great West Road. One of the best of these, Firestone, was half-demolished overnight in 1980 because the owners feared it might be 'listed'. Firestone became the Euston Arch of the eighties, and a new society was set up to fight for 1930s' buildings.

One thirties' monument which did survive was Battersea Power Station, a colossal 'cathedral of power' dominating Chelsea Reach. By the late seventies the conservationists were gaining ground. Billingsgate Market was saved (and converted into a hi-tech dealing floor). Covent Garden, scheduled for clearance, became the conserved heart of tourist London. The surviving dockland warehouses became stylish flats. Islington's Agricultural Hall – a St Pancras-style train-shed without a railway – became a 'business centre'.

London's new monuments – Lloyds, the NatWest tower, the Shell Centre, the Barbican – inspire little affection. The plodding pace of British planning has worked wonders to save London from further unwanted intruders – like Peter Palumbo's Mansion House Square block, rejected by the Government in 1984. Prince Charles became an ally of the conservationists and the bane of the modernists. Perhaps London has its share of monuments. The pleasures of London are found in modest streets and surviving neighbourhoods, like Soho, Fleet Street, Brixton market or the last lanes of the City. It is no accident that London's grandest architectural set piece is safely isolated at Greenwich. Londoners like the odd and the eccentric. Amidst the wilderness of the South Bank, the Oxo tower ('not advertising, just two noughts and a cross,' said the architects) is a monument not to architecture but to good humour and other humane values.

Covent Garden

Go to Covent Garden
before your arteries harden!
Oh, boy, believe me, that's a
genuine Piazza!

COVENT GARDEN

The medieval monks of Westminster Abbey would have been amazed. Their convent garden has done more than just lose an 'n'. The decades they spent in religious cultivation of vegetable plots, flowerbeds and orchards vanished long since. Today, over the grounds they worked so piously and lucratively (tradition has it that they sold the excess produce outside their gates) thousands of feet trample every day. The path that bisected their land, along which they walked deep in contemplation, has become one of London's liveliest streets: Long Acre. Black cabs play dodgems as they whisk their fares to the theatres close by; people spill out in throngs from the underground station; and The Body Shop, one of the 1980s' great success stories, lures passers-by through its glossy portals headlong into an agreeable narcissism.

Yet it was as recently as 1974 that the link between the two ages was broken. Until then a close-knit community still thrived on the sale of fruit and vegetables and attendant services. When the market moved out to Nine Elms many of the locals' livelihoods went with it. Families were split up as some moved on to new jobs and others stayed behind, ageing and jobless. London has largely these people to thank for what remains of Covent Garden's past. Supported by a public keenly interested in conservation after the more heinous acts of the sixties, they made a stand for the market and their homes when the GLC and the property developers tried to bring in the bulldozers. And they won.

The old community of the market – barrow boys racing up Long Acre, hustle and bustle throughout the night, pubs open late – has gone forever. A new community of about 5,000 has emerged though it will probably never be as close. Only a few of these are the wealthy who snap up the luxury flats.

Most are the market veterans or incoming young families of different nationalities living in council or housing association blocks not immediately obvious to passers-through. These flats are being modernised by Covent Garden's Housing Project – most were without heating systems and bathrooms. The Seven Dials Club in Earlham Street is a focal point for this community. Here you can sit down with a quiet pint for under a pound (unheard of elsewhere) or leave your children in a crèche. The Community Association and the Forum of Representatives, a specially elected body, act as watchdogs against the more money-grabbing development plans and have achieved a lot. There is still a lot to do. Covent Garden has no decent supermarket – if you run out of toothpaste, you'll end up with the healthy, myrhh-impregnated kind, not to everybody's taste after all; it has no decent park; and there aren't enough pedestrian crossings. The chaotic roads are a nightmare for children and adults alike.

This community is now entirely incidental to the covered market, though there are still a few people left who were trading in 1912 when George Bernard Shaw penned the famous meeting between Eliza Doolittle, the local flower girl, and the arrogant Professor Higgins under St Paul's portico. The stallholders trading today are a different breed altogether. Few, if any, are locals, but they are some of London's most striking 'alternative' people. They wouldn't like to think Norman Tebbit told them to, but they have certainly 'got on their bikes', creating beautiful craftworks, some of a really individual nature. These are pricey, mainly because renting a stall at Covent Garden is pricey. It is possible to buy the same item from the same person more cheaply at London's other markets, for instance Camden Lock. However, their clocks, glassware, jewellery, knitwear, puppets, mobiles and terrariums are popular both with tourists and English visitors, and with the bright young executives working close by in advertising, market-research agencies and the like.

Covent Garden has always been popular for its specialist shops: Chippendale himself set up shop in Long Acre, and when Sherlock Holmes went to Dartmoor on the scent of the Hound of the Baskervilles he sent to Stanfords in Long Acre for a detailed map of the moor. He could have done just that today. The Bead Shop and Buttonbox are irresistible to the magpies among us; but for those with money to burn, The Doll's House in the market's basement is stunning. Dolls' houses the size of a big television set cost up to £950 a throw and the tiniest, thimble-sized chair, a fiver. Most people go in here to gawp, but if you take a vicarious pleasure in watching others buy what you can't afford, you may see Mr and Mrs Hamilton-Cartwright buying something for Sarah-Jane (lucky Sarah-Jane): Mrs H-C stares at the cabinet containing dolls' furniture; 'Look at that darling piano,' she sighs. 'Actually, they're virginals,' says Mr H-C, but piano or virginals they buy it for £64.40. They may have bought an equally darling rocking horse at £40 – or they could have really splashed out and bought a full-sized version from Naturally British for a cool £916.55.

We can't all afford such treats. But it seems that most of us can still afford the pleasure of eating and dining out. Covent Garden is a popular meeting-place for many Londoners and every evening after work young girls with bobs and long earrings await their chums outside the underground station. Where will they find to talk in comfort? It takes forever to struggle up to the bar and order a drink in most pubs around about and you have to get in at 5.30 to have even a fighting chance of a seat. The Lamb and Flag is about the worst, a shame as it is a splendid place otherwise. In fact, it's surprising to reflect that it has if anything lived down its past. It used to be called the Bucket of Blood on account of the popular bare-knuckle boxing matches it held. Even bloodier, an assassination attempt was made here on John Dryden: the Duchess of Portsmouth, convinced he had libelled her, sent her agents to dispense with him. Happily they failed, but the event is still marked in the Lamb and Flag on 19 December ('Dryden Night').

If you want somewhere to sit down though, it's worth

trying the Lemon Tree behind the Coliseum. The Welsh Harp around the corner is equally pleasant. It is the orchestra's 'green room'. Bassoon players have been observed downing three pints in the 15-minute interval before hurtling back to their pit.

What visitors love most about Covent Garden and possibly what it is most renowned for today is its street entertainment. The buskers have taken over where the banter of the old market traders left off. Samuel Pepys would have done a double-take if he could have seen the same Punch and Judy shows he saw in 1662 still taking place in the same spot: St Paul's portico. Street artists are back at last. Anything from Indian dancing to escapology to fire-eating to juggling to robotics goes. Even better, the audiences are finally giving in to the natural exhibitionism that underlies the famous English reserve and joining in the acts with gusto.

Some acts are dire (who wants to hear 'The Boxer' mauled again?) but most aren't. To hear the Chinese folk musicians is enough to make anyone want to career around the piazza – but they are professionals. And, when Noise of Minstrels aren't demonstrating their medieval instruments to bemused passers-by, they're playing in the Barbican and National Theatre foyers. Other buskers are on the dole because their acts don't bring in enough money to live off. This means that they do *not* like to reveal either their identities or their earnings to journalists as in the past the tax office has got on to performers to declare their ill-gotten wages! 'Well, how much do *you* earn then?' retort the Officials – a delightfully over-the-top comedy duo. 'Do you realise we've all queued from six in the morning to get these bloody slots?' Noise of Minstrels admitted that on a really good summer's day they could get £60 for one show, provided they had a bottler to collect as they performed. But even this isn't a great deal when it's divided up.

Busking may be Covent Garden's most conspicuous element. It is an extraordinary fact that probably the most inconspicuous but also the most important element is the residential multi-racial community. Perhaps this is why many people dismiss Covent Garden as 'touristy' and 'trendy' implying that it has no real substance. And yet every element of London life is present in Covent Garden: the well-off and the poor exist side by side. In King Street near the piazza the eighties have brought us back an old legacy: the homeless and down and out. Punks come to earn a fiver having their photographs taken by tourists. Buskers come to supplement their unemployment benefit. Artisans come to sell their home-made wares upon which they depend. Covent Garden is in short a hybrid of all that is frivolous, industrious, sad and hopeful in our lives. Trendy it may be, but dull it certainly isn't.

FLEET STREET

From my window in the new *Daily Telegraph* office at South Quay, I look out upon sixteen tower cranes. The reconstruction of London's Docklands, they say, is the biggest capital city development anywhere in the world. How strange that Fleet Street, arguably until a year or so ago the most industrially retarded of all our trades, should now find much of itself in London's most modern quarter.

The history of this metamorphosis can be written in a couple of sentences. Intransigent dockers closed the London docks. Intransigent printers drove newspapers out of Fleet Street into the vacuum the dockers had left.

The surprising thing is not that Fleet Street has come so suddenly to an end, but that its obstinately unchanging form survived for as long as it did. It was not so much the newspapers' economics, which were crazy, but the sheer physical absurdity of such industrial activity in central London. A Street of Adventure, Sir Philip Gibbs called it. In reality it was a factory zone. Moreover it had been planted across a main highway through Central London, linking the City with the West End.

Through the daylight hours the lorries rolled in from the docks and elsewhere, delivering to the street and off the street mountains of newsprint rolls. At night the street was thronged with vans lined up to gallop early editions to the mainline railway stations. Every surrounding street was a car park for Fleet Street's workers. From basements in and around the street came a sound not to be heard anywhere else in inner London – the thundering of heavy machinery, the printing presses.

Covent Garden, with its flower, fruit and vegetable market, was far less obtrusive, but it was banished to Battersea on the grounds that the market's lorries impeded traffic. This innocent and silent market off the Strand was perceived, with all the foolish prejudice which afflicted postwar town planners, to be out of place, a traffic nuisance, an enemy of conformity and of real estate.

Its dismissal to Battersea was foolish because every great capital should indulge in its midst a reminder of our links to the natural things of life. Billingsgate and its fish were also called upon to move. Yet Fleet Street's noisy complex was indulged. The presses were too heavy and the press was too strong for the planners to prevail.

Like Broadway in New York, Fleet Street had become more a symbol than a stable of its trade. The *Times* was never there, but first in Printing House Square off Blackfriars; and then with the *Sunday Times* and the *Guardian* in relatively far-off Gray's Inn Road. Among the nationals only the *Daily Express* and its companions along with the *Daily Telegraph* had roots in Fleet Street itself. Lord Camrose rebuilt the *Telegraph* building in the late 1920s. Lord Beaverbrook, lower down the hill but not to be outshone, went for the Dallas look. Their frontages at least will live on for a time. After more than half a century they deserve to be on one of the lists which preserve historic buildings. There will also remain in Fleet Street the great agencies of Reuter and the Press Association which fittingly, since they are expected to be reliable rather than expressive, occupy a building of unremarkable exterior.

In truth, what gave Fleet Street its character before the war was not the nationals but the host of newspapers outside London which kept small offices there. In the thirties there were scores of them. They were the sources of the 'London Letter' columns, long since abandoned by progressive news-papers. Though sometimes occupying no more than a single room, they were salutary reminders that although the press lords spoke loudest, theirs was not the only voice. When they went and the big blocks became monopolies, much of the Street's character went as well.

American visitors to London are drawn to Fleet Street —

not least for the matchless picture they get from different angles of St Paul's Cathedral on the hill beyond. 'Where's the Cheshire Cheese?' they ask. Once there, sawdust under their feet, they appear shyly and unaccountably to seek every drink except the draught beer for which the place is renowned.

An industry with no fixed hours in the twenty-four has need of watering holes. Some of the most progressive companies in Britain today go for canteens in which directors and office boys eat side by side. Fleet Street, which until quite recently has been the nation's least progressive industry, always worked on those lines. White collars and blue collars drank together. It was a fraternity.

Journalists are by nature gregarious. Like the barristers who live close to Fleet Street, journalists have always profited by friendly association with their own kind. It is just possible that, indirectly, newspaper readers have profited from this as well.

With the end of the Street, newspapers are going to be far better printed, almost certainly more regular in delivery and, in theory at least, much less expensive. Yet great newspapers are founded on their contents, not their appearances. The computer revolution which has brought about the end of the Street will not of itself make newspapers wiser, more accurate or better informed.

There is, however, no call to mourn for Fleet Street. The City of London, of which it is part, will not for long leave its valuable acreage unoccupied. Soon there will be new blocks towering over the street, housing those engaged in making money rather than newspapers. There will be fewer pubs and more wine bars. It will become a far more respectable neighbourhood.

My vision of the Street was formed very late in life by a beautiful girl who was star columnist on a Washington newspaper. A mutual friend had called me from America and begged me to take her out to lunch.

She came to the newspaper office punctually, gave her name and said she had a lunch appointment with me. Somehow the

'*White collars and blue collars drank together.*'

front office contrived to mislay her in the confusion. When, some minutes later, I caught up with her downstairs, she was sitting smiling hopefully on a pile of disused newspapers near the entrance.

We walked out. I began to apologise. We had never met before. She slipped her arm through mine comfortingly and said, 'Not to worry. Never forget the great newspapers of the world come out of what look like slums.' Never a truer word said. We had a lovely lunch. That *was* Fleet Street.

SOHO

Soho at first sight is a disappointment. It doesn't have the screaming glitz of Las Vegas or the spectacular criminality of New York's 42nd Street. As big city entertainment districts go, Soho is subdued, quaint, almost countrified, which is a great part of its charm. As with most things English, Soho is subtle. By midnight it's a graveyard, a sleepy collection of olde worlde buildings. A few furtive-looking Bangladeshis scuttle out of the 'model upstairs' doorways. (Look for them in St Ann's Court.) Otherwise the place is deserted. By eleven the pubs, theatres, strip clubs and a lot of the restaurants are closed. If you're still out looking for a good time, you've got a couple of clip joints, one or two noisy young discos and a couple of excellent but expensive jazz venues to choose from. So much for night life. For visitors used to Paris and New York the small hours in Soho are awfully quiet.

The clip joints are to be avoided unless you are a masochist, but if you like being robbed and maybe even beaten up, it might be for you. At the sleaziest end of the scale is the Golden Girl in Meard Street. They will promise you the moon through their barbed-wire window but woe betide you if you come in and insist on getting what you've paid for. The girls in there are men and big strong men at that and they have only one aim in mind – getting hold of your money, which they do, no holds barred.

Munro's in Greek Street is a more upmarket rip-off. There you have champagne hostesses you can drink with and perhaps make private arrangements with for a phenomenal price. Strip theatres, peepshows and models are straightforward, you pay what they ask at the door and that's it. There are, as the barkers say, no hidden extras. But any place that advertises girls and drinks in combination is a place to steer clear of unless you want to pay a lot for very little.

The sex industry in Soho is tatty, badly done rubbish. The jazz scene on the other hand has some standards. The best people in the world play at Ronnie Scott's in Frith Street. The food is bad, drinks and admission are not particularly cheap, the audience is mostly middle-aged and sycophantic, but the music can be wonderful. If you go to the downstairs bar, you can get a flavour of backstage, eavesdrop on musicians in intense discussion about music or watch them being the wild, crazy people some jazz musicians like to see themselves as. It makes a pleasant change from the insipidly polite crowd upstairs. At Piazza Express in Dean Street you can also hear excellent jazz. The names are not as superluminary but neither are the prices.

By day Soho is an island of real food set amid oceans of junk. To the north there's Oxford Street, full of fast food, badly made shoes and clothes guaranteed to fall apart in a month. To the south Leicester Square is chock-a-block with every franchise you can name – Kentucky Fried Chicken, Wimpy, McDonalds, Pancake House, Baskin Robbin. Running in a north–south line between these two emporiums of soulless grey pap is Soho's Berwick Street, home of fresh fruits, vegetables, pastas, cheeses and sausages. We have the Italians to thank for this.

On Old Compton Street you can get some of the best cream cakes in London served in trendy cafés where the conversation is arty – everybody comments on each other's scripts or talks about the last show they were in. Patisserie Valerie is best for eavesdropping or posing, whichever your predilection. If you're a real cake-lover, visit Maison Bertaux. The cakes at Patisserie Valerie look pretty but they're not that tasty.

If you want to go out for a meal you have a lot to choose from – Chinese, French, Indian, Malaysian, Greek, Italian, Hungarian, and in every price range. If you're looking for something edible for under £5 a head, try Il Pollo in Old Compton Street or the Lorelei in Bateman Street. They are both in the fine Italian tradition of serving fresh food made from scratch (as opposed to the powdered custard, tinned soup and grease tradition upheld by many English cafés). Soho is a blessed exception to the fact that second-rate eating is still rife in London despite the advent of the foodies.

If you want a drink, the Crown and Two Chairmen in Dean Street is not recommended. The bar is small and you can't get to it due to the crowds. Although the barmaids have been known to be hospitable, the service is generally very slow. In fact in most Soho pubs on week nights between 5.30 and 7.00 pm and at lunch you will be hard-pressed to get to the bar, let alone order or hear yourself think. You are likely to have some overgrown ego from film or advertising bellowing in your ear or spilling beer over you. The pubs in Soho are crawling with pretentious media types except on Sunday when it's like death and that's why it's nice. Go to the Dog 'n'Duck for Sunday lunch and you can have a drink in peace and quiet and enjoy a sense of being part of the family of indigenous oddballs; the emaciated geriatric strippers in North-American Indian gear, elderly alcoholics who seem to have stepped out of a Noël Coward set, and most of the ageing queens also to be seen at the Golden Lion or French's every night. It's not a young scene but it has its own quirky charm. If on the other hand you're trying to chat up young art students, try the Soho Brasserie – St Martin's art school hangs out there. The villains (if you're after a villain) used to congregate at the Swiss, but now the Swiss is closed they can be found just about anywhere around the area. Try the Blue Posts in Berwick Street.

If you're looking for something fresh and wholesome, Soho Square is as near ask you'll get in Soho. On a fine summer afternoon you'll find kids, tourists, pigeons, squabbling winos, pimply young men of no fixed address pestering the office girls, and office girls out showing off their legs and complaining about the perverts all out together enjoying the trees, the grass, the well-kept Regency buildings and of course, the sun.

Soho packs in unspeakable tat and enormous excellence and sophistication cheek by jowl. On top of that it's a sane, friendly place when you compare it to Pigalle or the Reeper-bahn. Wildly varied and often extremely talented people live together with the relative tolerance and civility that London, in spite of all its problems, still seems better able to provide than most of the world's other great cities.

HAMPSTEAD

Hampstead is not just a place but a state of mind. Every western city with any pretensions to city-ness has a Hampstead, an enclave where the great and the goodly live, high achievers in the world of the arts, music, publishing, media, politics, the law, medicine, most of them caring and concerned, right- and left-thinking people, who seldom flaunt their wealth and success.

They don't hide themselves away, like those capitalist sheep in Mayfair or Knightsbridge, turning their backs on the world, nor do they come out and take part in those rather passing trends and fashions which so occupy their flashier brethren in Chelsea. Hampstead folk are cleverer and more calculating. They put their names to petitions which they know will look good, or sign letters which are bound to end up in the *Times*, the *Guardian* or the *Independent*.

They're not daft, these Hampstead folk. Why else did they all flock to what is today the nicest, the most favoured London enclave?

Architecturally there are finer squares elsewhere in London, handsomer houses, more impressive terraces, but what Hampstead has got is hills. No chunk of inner London has this geographical advantage. Nor has any area, throughout urban London, got the majestic space of Hampstead Heath, London's greatest living lung. No wonder Hampstead types feel pretty happy with themselves, looking down their noses from the heights.

The name Hampstead comes from the Saxon word 'Hamstede', meaning homestead, as in farm homestead. Until well after the Middle Ages, farming was about the only activity there, especially pig farming. By the sixteenth century it had become a small community, known for its laundresses.

'Hampstead folk . . . sign letters which are bound to end up
in the Times.'

London gentry, including royalty, sent their washing up to the heights of Hampstead where a colony of washerwomen had established itself, using the natural springs on the wild, scrubby Heath, as well as various streams, such as the Fleet, which flow down into the Thames in London. (The Fleet is now underground, so don't bother looking for it.) On a dry day, it was said that the top of Hampstead was like a snow-capped mountain, all those lines of linen, flapping in the wind.

In the early eighteenth century, Hampstead became a fashionable watering place and people flocked to spas near Well Walk which were said to have medicinal qualities. The first period of Hampstead development then began, around Church Row and the High Street. Things became a little rougher when a racecourse and fairground on the Heath attracted a rowdier element, but by the late nineteenth century life was more respectable, the residents more refined, wealthy professional men crept up from the City, and successful publishers moved in from Bloomsbury, all settling down with their families and servants. There were also a lot of artists and writers, a traditional element in Hampstead life for the last 150 years, from Constable and Keats, to John Le Carré and Margaret Drabble.

Church Row is a good way to begin a Hampstead tour, as it's very impressive and near the tube station. Turn right at the end of it, just past the parish church, and into Holly Walk, working your way through the back squares and lanes up to Whitestone Pond. You don't see any shops or bijou caffs this way. You can pretend it's still the eighteenth century.

There's a famous pub at the top, Jack Straw's Castle, a fine building, but not really recommended, as you're now entering tourist country. The Bull and Bush, the Spaniards and the Flask over in Highgate are four well known hostelries which form a ring round the Heath.

Cut right across the main road and on to the Heath proper, breathe in deeply, admire that sweeping view, ponder on such a marvel being there, open and free for all to enjoy. Poor old

New York, with that crummy bit of concrete-lined Central Park. No major city in the world has such a rural pearl.

It is hard to believe, but Hampstead Heath is now four times the size, over 800 acres today, that it was in 1871 when an Act of Parliament first took it over for the people. Bits still get added all the time, even if it's only a few acres on the edge as another garden or bit of parkland gets taken over.

You may scoff, as many cynical Londoners do, at those Hampstead types who are for ever running action groups, but it has been their commitment to the Heath, saving it from developers, obstructing short-sighted politicians, which has given us our finest urban park. In fact it could be argued that Hampstead Heath is the greatest achievement of any preservation lobby anywhere.

In the middle of the Heath is Kenwood House, one of Hampstead's three major houses open to the public. (The others are Keats House and Fenton House.) It's an Adam masterpiece, architecturally speaking, and inside there are other sorts of masterpieces, by Rembrandt, Vermeer, Gainsborough. You'll rub your eyes in amazement. A country house, in its own parkland, four miles from the centre of London, yet utterly tranquil and dignified, stashed full with treasures. The cafeteria in the coach house, with a fairly large menu, though the coffee is not as good as the much smaller caff in nearby Golders Hill. (Don't forget, by the way, that the Heath is a funny old shape, with lots of extensions. Try to buy the map, which was priced 50p in the GLC days, written by Ralph Wade.)

Highgate guards the other side of the Heath, a miniature version of Hampstead, with not as many attractions or crowds, but it does have its very own cemetery, a Victorian folly, beautifully overgrown in its older section, where there are memorials to Michael Faraday, Rowland Hill, George Eliot, and John Galsworthy. In the newer section lies Karl Marx, popular with visiting Russian and Chinese delegations. Count the cameras.

Head back across the Heath, aiming for Downshire Hill,

then turn right up the High Street, and you're once again in the Hampstead heartlands, this time amongst the shops and restaurants, students and tourists, foreigners and phoneys. Take a peep into Flask Walk, buy some books or have a drink, or pop into Perrins Court, on the other side of the road, and pick up the latest edition of the *Hampstead and Highgate Express*, the best local paper anywhere on the island. It will make good reading for your journey home on the tube. But ignore the acres of estate agent prose. The prices will only depress you. That's about the only sad thing today, in Happy Hampstead . . .

BEDFORD PARK

On 17 December 1881, the *St James's Gazette* published a twenty-three stanza 'Ballad of Bedford Park', in which an anonymous poet poked gentle fun at the newly established garden suburb of Bedford Park, 'Where men may lead a chaste, correct/Aesthetical existence.'

This, the first planned garden suburb, had been initiated by Jonathan Carr (1845–1915) in 1875. Carr was a speculative developer; he had dabbled in cloth merchandising and fancied himself as a dilettante. He bought three Georgian houses built by the brothers Bedford on a twenty-four-acre estate at Turnham Green, without proper backing to lay it out, yet he managed to expand from this nucleus by acquiring more land, and by 1883 the estate comprised 113 acres with 490 houses. Nevertheless, his finances were still very shaky; as soon as he bought land he was obliged to mortgage it, and in an attempt to solve his problems he sold land to a company, Bedford Park Ltd, in 1881. This failed five years later, with half the land still unbuilt upon, and its assets were acquired by the Bedford Park Estate Ltd who then broke up the estate by selling land piecemeal, leaving others to build houses and flats in a variety of styles.

Such an unpromising start must prompt the question why Bedford Park quickly earned a reputation for civilised living among the ever-increasing number of writers, actors and artists who came to settle there in the 1880s, when it was at its first apogee of fashion.

The Aesthetic Movement of the 1870s had created among some members of the London middle class a taste for a simpler life style, in revulsion against the vulgarity of heavy, ornate mahogany furniture and the debased over-elaborate architecture of High Victorianism. They also sought a more rural setting, away from the fogs and filth of central London but, as in our own day, with good rail connections. Above all, the houses were both cheap and architect-designed.

Carr's first choice of architect was an archpriest of the Aesthetic Movement, Edward Godwin, who held advanced views on modern women's clothing, which he argued should be more hygienic and rational in design. He was also a protagonist of the 'art' furniture movement, basing his designs on the simple elegance of Japanese prototypes. But Carr was none too scrupulous in his dealings, and also demanded rigorous adherence to strict cost limits on his house designs. Godwin resigned and was replaced by Richard Norman Shaw in 1877, who was responsible for such key buildings as the church of St Michael and All Angels, and opposite it, the Tabard Inn. These, and his ingenious series of terrace, detached and semi-detached houses (notably those in Woodstock Road), were meant for mass-replication, and were designed in the charming red-brick and white-painted woodwork of the Queen Anne Revival style, called by Mark Girouard the embodiment of 'sweetness and light'. Other architects also contributed designs, including Godwin's assistant, Maurice B. Adams, E. J. May and William Wilson.

Both Norman Shaw and Carr had good connections, and were able to publicise the new venture extensively, and this was an important factor in its success. Carr's brother, Comyns Carr, art critic and publisher, was a very useful ally. The houses are charming to look at, and early photographs show wide, winding roads planted with young trees, the houses bounded by, for the most part, clapboard fences, although the grander mansions sport white wooden palisades, with the elegantly curved and finialled iron spacers over the gates that are now coming back into fashion.

There is still a village atmosphere in Bedford Park. The trees, mostly limes, planes and chestnuts, have matured beautifully; some were there before the estate was developed, others have died or been felled at the request of dendrophobic householders who have persuaded the local councils that their roots were undermining the foundations. During the Second World War, some houses as well as the Chiswick School of Art were bombed, but the councils of Ealing and Hounslow have been, until recently, even more destructive than Hitler. They have demolished, among other fine houses, Carr's own grandiloquent Tower House (the expense of which contributed to his financial difficulties), and only after a hard struggle by the Bedford Park Society (formed in 1963, and known affectionately as 'BedSock'), aided by the Victorian Society, were two conservation areas formed in 1969 and 1970, which cover most of the old Bedford Park estate.

The houses come in a great variety of ground plan, elevation and size. Some are hardly bigger than delightful dolls' houses, others boast impracticably large reception and bedrooms. A peculiarity of the true Bedford Park house is the absence of a cellar; those built post-1887, however, do possess this necessity. It may seem strange that the artistic fraternity should be thought so abstemious as not to need a cellar for laying down choice vintages, but the answer lies in the additional cost involved in their construction. It is also a sad fact that Bedford Park houses are not always well founded; not a few have suffered from subsidence, being built almost straight on top of the subsoil. This is slyly alluded to in *The Ballad*: 'Now he who loves aesthetic cheer/And does not mind the damp/May come and read Rossetti here/By a Japanesc-y lamp./While 'Arry shouts to Hemma/Say, 'ere's a blooming lark!/Them's the biled lobster 'ouses/As folks calls "Bedford Park!"' In another verse, we have a reference to 'stained and polished floors', which anticipates the sanded and sealed floors in vogue today. None of the principal architects had time to supervise the building of every house, and the quality of workmanship, materials and finish is erratic, to say the least. Garden plots, too, with a few exceptions, are minuscule in comparison with those in more monotonous neighbouring suburbs.

Despite its shortcomings, Bedford Park presents a distinctive and attractive face. It has suffered hard times. Instead of distinguished painters and writers like W.B. Yeats, his father and brother (both painters), the actor William Terriss and the playwright Pinero, or the briefly notorious anarchist Sergius Stepniak, who lived there in the 1880s and 1890s, many houses have become flats and rooming houses (a process slowly being reversed).

Poor refugees from Poland, Greece and Armenia settled in during the 1940s and after. Even quite grand houses could still be bought cheaply in the early 1960s. Now it has become fashionable and much sought-after by the discerning. Members of the princely Galitzin family rub shoulders, metaphorically at least, with Angela Rippon and John Hurt. Architects, art historians, writers, journalists, distinguished solicitors, financiers, and those new financial 'aristos' – accountants, are thick on the ground. Village-style shops cling on to a livelihood; there are flourishing Bedford Park Festivals and 'Green Days' held on Acton Green every first Saturday in June. Even more eccentric are the dog birthday parties held there occasionally by groups of manic kuonophiliacs. The Tabard Inn has recently revived seasons of intimate studio theatre. Bedford Park flourishes again.

LITTLE VENICE

A mile and a quarter northwest of Marble Arch (yes, along the Edgware Road, believe it or not) lies an area which a historian described in 1853 as 'a city of palaces' and the critical Pevsner, eighty years later, as 'one of the most attractive Early Victorian tree and stucco landscapes of London.' No book on London would be complete without a visit to the scene Robert Browning looked onto for twenty-five years and which has since drawn others of the great and good as residents.

The maps call it Maida Vale, a misnomer since it rises to a hill which is in fact seventy-six feet above high watermark. Maida Vale proper, by which I mean lower down and farther along the Edgware Road, was a dreadful place to live when I was young. In 1887 the now-forgotten novelist, Frank Danby, had described it in *A Maida Vale Romance* as full of rich, vulgar Jews (she could say that, being Jewish herself — in truth Julia Frankau, mother and grandmother of novelists). By 1914 the richer of these had moved to Hampstead (or Park Lane) and been replaced by those who could not afford the luxury of stucco, so the district was very down-at-heel. And there were ladies in the streets to whom, young as I was, I could see it would not do for me to talk. To make things worse, there was a dingy canal along which coal-carrying barges shuffled under clouds of smoke.

Then a miracle occurred. Perhaps some twenty years ago an estate-agent's copywriter, groping for something better to say about a house by the canal than that it was in Maida Vale, was inspired to describe it as being in 'Little Venice'. Since then everything has changed and a pleasurable hour may well be spent studying this oasis off what once was Watling Street and is now the unspeakable Edgware Road.

'*And there were ladies in the streets, to whom, young as I was, I could see it would not do for me to talk.*'

Little Venice, like its serene sister city, should of course be approached by water. It can be, but that would mean starting from Camden Town and journeying along a canal even drearier than the Brenta. Instead, we will take a bus to the Hero of Maida, an inn by the Maida Hill tunnel of the Regent's canal from which the district came by its original name. The hero was Sir John Stuart, a general of the Napoleonic wars who had a fortunate, rather than heroic, encounter with the French at San Pietro di Maida in Calabria. The inn has been replaced by a pub which need not detain us (there will be more agreeable stopping places) but from it we may look down the Vale. Where we are standing is the point at which John Nash (referred to as 'John 'Beau' Nash' in the literature fed to the waterbus tourists) began the adventure that was to lead him to the creation of Regent's Park. After a disastrous start the canal was at last opened to traffic in 1820.

Unlike the other Venice, which resisted church influence for a thousand years, the whole of Paddington has been church territory since Edward VI gave it to the Bishop of London. Its government has long been delegated to a kind of executive arm called Chesterton's and, at the time of writing, the church's proprietorial rights are being relinquished to those of the inhabitants who can afford to pay for them; if they cannot so afford, others are found who can. This is the explanation of the scaffolding which covers a large proportion of the buildings; before long the whole area will have been restored to its original glory and all that will remain of the 400-year church rule will be the names of bishops, such as Randolph and Blomfield, or their better-off lessees, such as a Miss Warwick (pay no attention to more fanciful derivations of street names to which the inhabitants are addicted).

From the Hero of Maida we follow the main road, passing a few shops, cross Maida Avenue on the south bank of the canal, go over the bridge, with its quaint shop which anywhere else in Europe would be a café, and turn left into Blomfield Road. We are soon barred from the towpath, and thus protected from the 'barge people' whose arrival was regarded with apprehension by the opponents of Nash's scheme, but can walk close to the canal with little difficulty. We are in the street that captivated Pevsner, the canal here being lined on both sides by plane trees and (after a few blocks of flats on the south bank) pretty villas, mostly stucco of the 1830s. The seemingly Byzantine building across the canal is the Catholic Apostolic Church, founded in 1832 by the followers of Edward Irving who believed in the impending end of the world; they are said to be discouraged by subsequent events (or lack of them) and their future is in doubt.

We soon reach another bridge, originally a weighbridge to which Byron is said to have dragged a reluctant John Murray to show him the spot where a publisher had drowned himself (it would be pleasant to be able to provide a source for this much-repeated story but myths abound in Little Venice). Here we cross Warwick Avenue and enter a well-kept garden on our left. We have momentarily left church property, and the reigning authority, in the form of the Westminster City Council, have pointedly called it Rembrandt Garden to stress an association with Amsterdam rather than with Venice. (If the district has to be called after another city, Amsterdam, let us face it, might be more appropriate, but the tastes of property buyers have to be considered.) Ahead of us is a triangular pool from which a branch of the canal leads off to the left towards a basin beside Paddington Station. Up until now we have been walking beside the Regent's Canal, which would have led to Regent's Park and the London docks, but ahead of us it has become the Grand Union Canal and from here we could travel by water to Manchester or any part of England. Well, almost any part. In front of us is an island planted with willow, lit up at regatta times, and, on the right, a barge used as a picture gallery and another as a restaurant. On the left, the south side of the triangle, is the terminus of the waterbus we might have taken from Camden Lock (a competitive barge docks a little farther on). The houses rising from this bank are in Warwick Crescent where, at number

19, Robert Browning lived. No sign of his habitation can be found and this side of the canal marks the beginning of a vast housing estate which recalls Mestre rather than Venice. Needless to say there is no sign of a café in the garden although there are two lavatories. We are in London, not Venice.

We therefore leave the garden and turn left along the splendid Warwick Avenue, scarcely a city of palaces, but with homes for the already well heeled and becoming more so every day. In one of these (three, to be accurate) lives the most spectacular of the Rothschilds. Turning down the first street to the left, Warwick Place, we find a small row of shops which includes one selling fine old garden ornaments; from it we can reach the celebrated Clifton Nurseries, property of Jacob Rothschild, although the main entrance is from the next street, Clifton Villas. There is also that rarity in London, a bookshop, and, next to it, a restaurant called Didier's where, if it is lunchtime, we can eat well, perhaps very well. For a much more modest lunch we could eat at the Warwick Castle; for something between the two we must wait five minutes.

St Saviour's church in Warwick Avenue, to which we now return, is no St Mark's but if Little Venice has a Piazza we are now in it. The modern church occupies a small part of the site of one of those huge Victorian structures, which has now been demolished, and the rest of the site is now occupied by a block of flats. A worthy intention and who are we to criticise the carrying out? The structure in front of the church is a ventilating shaft for the underground station, not the remains of its campanile. Passing to the left of the church we come to Formosa Street. Were we to turn left here, we would reach a hideous bridge leading to G.E. Street's St Mary Magdalene, built on a sloping dumping ground with none of its sides parallel, but, strangely enough, a triumphant success. However, we did not come to Paddington just to look at churches so we turn right, soon reaching the more interesting end of Formosa Street. Its few shops occupy what has been described as 'a grand but miniature urban block, its east and west façades stuccoed black, with giant Corinthian pilasters.'

Opposite the shops is the Prince Albert with its four bars, including a Ladies' and a series of etched glass screens, unsurpassed in London and seldom equalled.

Turning right at the end of Formosa Street we pass the Colonnade Hotel which bears a blue plaque recording that Sigmund Freud lived there; in fact he spent but a few days there before being carried off for an operation from which he never recovered. We are now back in Warwick Avenue and, if exhausted, can reach any part of London from the Bakerloo underground station. However, a few minutes' walk along Clifton Gardens, to the left (or a number 6 bus if one happens to present itself) will lead to a shopping area with five shops selling greengrocery, an ironmonger and a post office. It also contains a serious Italian restaurant called Romano's which has maintained its standards despite being in London, and is said to have done so for many years. And, amazingly enough, there is a café which might almost be in Vienna (a 'cafay', as opposed to a 'caif', for which we should have to go to the Edgware Road). Just off this remarkable street is the Windsor Castle, small and crowded inside, but with an admirable display of flowers outside. Presiding over everything is the seat of the Church's delegates, bearing the name 'Chestertons' over the door.

To the north is the rest of the Maida Vale estate, hardly worth exploring today, despite the occasional worthwhile find it offers. Scaffolding is everywhere from which eventually the city of palaces will no doubt re-emerge. Distance from Nash's canal does not seem to preclude the magic designation 'Little Venice' which our children may well see extended to Kilburn. Meanwhile, God help us, we are back at the Edgware Road.

Greenwich Hospital

A trip down the river to Greenwich
is as good for you as spinach.
Wren's Hospital is beautiful past telling –
and both spinach and Greenwich will improve your spelling.

SOUTH OF THE RIVER

It was a choice between south London or divorce — there seemed no other way you could reconcile my wife's work in Epsom and mine in central London. And since we had only been married for a few months and were very keen to remain together, it had to be south London. I practised repeating the two fateful words to myself, trying to get used to the alien concept they represented. But it was no good — the notion of 'south of the river' only called up the same doom-laden feelings as phrases like 'the empty quarter', 'the frozen north', or 'the Gulag Archipelago'. And so it was with a heavy heart that I prepared to say goodbye to my small terrace in Kentish Town — so near to everything worth getting to. Once a north Londoner, always one.

To my surprise, we found the ideal house in south London straightaway. It was a wide, brick-built Edwardian semi in Tooting, with a garden cunningly designed and planted to make all surrounding buildings invisible. It was even decorated in a style which suited us. There was only one question which niggled a little as we drove away from the viewing in a glow of amazement. Why were the charming occupants sleeping in a small back bedroom rather than the light and spacious first-floor room at the front of the house? Their own explanation was that they had moved to give way to guests one weekend, and had never troubled to move back. I rang the local councillor to ask him about the area. A good place to live, he assured me — the only thing to remember is that it's close to Bedford Hill. Now I'd heard about prostitution in Soho and Shepherd's Market and King's Cross, of course — they were on the north bank. So he had to explain that Bedford Hill is south London's notorious red-light area. Check it out around 11 p.m., he suggested.

Parked nearby, we watched in fascination. The street corner opposite our ideal home was as busy as the taxi rank at Victoria Station. Down one road came the girls – in furs, in fishnets, in minis, in leathers; along the other came the punters – in Escorts, in Allegros, in Maxis, in Volvos. The door would open, a girl would climb in, the door would slam, the engine would rev up, and away they would roar in triumph and anticipation. Now we knew what had driven those respectable citizens out of their front bedroom. On the way home, dejection fought with my satisfaction at this speedy confirmation of the dreadfulness of south London.

Well, that's about the most exciting thing which has happened to us in south London. With no great enthusiasm, we bought a jerry-built Victorian terraced house, similar to thousands of others, and did our best to settle in and look on the bright side. We soon noticed, however, that there was a significant social change taking place around us – the Sloanification of the south. This was 1982, and house prices in Kensington, Chelsea and Fulham had just begun pushing some of their traditional inhabitants out across the Thames. From one week to the next, the place seemed to be increasingly infested with green wellies, bodywarmers, Alice bands, Dalmation dogs and unselfconscious, upper-crust voices. In the mornings, the approaches to Chelsea and Battersea Bridges were clogged with Golf GTIs and the smallest BMWs as this tribe returned to their natural habitat for the working day. It wasn't long before they had earned themselves the sobriquet 'Soanlies' – when mentioning their new address, of which they felt slightly ashamed, they would forever remind people that ''s only ten minutes from Sloane Square.' Estate agents have started calling parts of Battersea 'south Chelsea' or 'Chelsea Reach'.

Our first direct experience of Soanlies came soon after a couple moved into a house whose garden backed on to ours. They held a noisy garden-warming party one summer evening. Our next door neighbour's teenage daughter, no doubt trying to drown the braying and hooraying from the Simons and

'... the highest burglary rate in the country.'

Felicities, opened her bedroom window and switched Mike Oldfield to full volume. This soon proved overwhelming for the male half of the new couple, who, after several aggressive but ineffectual shouts of 'excuse me', turned up on our doorstep in tennis shorts, riding a bicycle and demanding plummily that we turn the music down. My wife gave him the half-minute ice-maiden treatment. Even after he'd found the right house and Mike Oldfield had subsided, the braying continued well into the night.

Still, we've learnt to live with this kind of thing and have even, armed with maps and interpreters, made some cautious social contact with the new tribe. Certain conveniences also seem to have been drawn in their wake, just as gulls and gannets might follow a cruise liner. All along Battersea Rise, Lavender Hill and Bellevue Road, there is a new crop of wine bars, boutiques, delicatessens and restaurants, which generally try too hard and charge too much. The bistros and pizza houses usually remind me of a quip in *Vogue* – that the only good restaurants south of the river are in France. But one shouldn't cavil; the area has become more varied and interesting. Why, the police tell us that it has the highest burglary rate in the country.

Will I ever be reconciled? Well, I doubt it. I remain convinced that the best parts of south London are those from which you can still see north London. On the north bank, after all, are to be found the head, heart and soul of the capital. Once the river has been crossed and you lose that splendid panorama of the north bank, you are in a lower, functional and unlovely section of the city. My heart always sinks a little as I cross Waterloo Bridge and enter the gloom; there is so little to look forward to. A glimpse of green on Clapham Common, perhaps, where the joggers weave between the dog turds, or a certain excitement on the streets of Brixton. You can climb out of the flatlands to Brockwell Park, Crystal Palace or Blackheath, of course, but their main virtue is that they allow you to gaze back to the north bank again. Grand buildings? Well, there's the Royal Naval College in Greenwich, and, and . . . oh, some of the largest blocks of flats in Europe, if you're into that sort of thing. No – south London, I'm afraid, is a twilight inner-city hinterland succeeded only by the pitiless infinities of places like Streatham, Catford, Collier's Wood and Croydon. When I stand sometimes and stare through a tangle of discarded crisp packets and fishing lines into the murky shallows of the ponds on Clapham Common, my mind returns mistily to the lake at Kenwood on Hampstead Heath on an autumn morning. One day, I'll be going back.

RICHMOND

Walk up the track from the Upper Richmond Road through the National Trust's Sheen Common and after a few hundred yards you'll come to a heavy iron gate set in the wall which divides the common from Richmond Park. Continue through and head due south. Away to the west the only building you can see is the spire of St Matthias' Church. Skirt Bog Lodge and keep going to the highest point of Sawyer's Hill, pausing before you get to Sidmouth Wood. Now look to your left and if you are lucky and the day is bright you will see the whole of London laid out before you with the sun glinting on the gold cross of the Dome of St Paul's. Near here Henry VIII is supposed to have stood, over 400 years ago, straining to see the smoke from the cannon at the Tower of London which would signal the execution of Anne Boleyn.

When you can tear yourself away from this prospect, head west to the Richmond Park gate opposite the Star and Garter Home for Disabled Ex-Servicemen, a vast red-brick monster though arguably the borough's best cause. Remind yourself that it is built on the site of the hotel where Charles Dickens invited Thackeray and Tennyson to join him to celebrate the publication of *David Copperfield*, and walk north past the Wick, where the theatrical family Mills (Sir John, Hayley, etc.) once lived and the Wick House built in 1772 for Sir Joshua Reynolds. Then gaze west across the Terrace Field and watch the Thames snaking through the meadows towards Twickenham. James Thomson, the poet who wrote 'Rule Britannia' described it in *The Seasons*. Everyone who writes about Richmond mentions this but no one ever quotes the words. It is because of this view that the capital of Virginia was named Richmond (though the American view is not half as good). If it's a clear day you will be able to distinguish the outline of Windsor Castle on the horizon.

It is often said that London is a series of villages but Richmond is the only part of London which feels like a town of consequence in its own right. Apart from the remarkable views it has a considerable history. Henry VII built a large royal palace here, though only a few bits remain – notably the Gate House. Elizabeth I lived and died in Richmond Palace. Shakespeare performed there. The Stuarts came mainly for the hunting, but it was a favourite retreat for the Hanoverians until George III clashed with the 'Vestry', the town's ruling body, who refused to sell him land for a new palace in 1769.

The motto of the modern tourism association is 'where the countryside comes to town', which is fair if inelegant. As you fly in to Heathrow (aircraft noise is the bane of Richmond,) look down and marvel at the great expanses of green: Richmond Park itself, Kew Gardens, Bushy Park, Hampton Court, and slicing through it some of the prettiest reaches of the Thames in London.

Richmond not only has the feel of a country town but also something of the raffishness of a resort. At various periods in its history that is exactly what it has been – a place where the city dwellers have come for a night out. Summer Saturday nights in the town still sometimes seem a little louche and local residents are constantly complaining about the rowdy gatherings on the Green which has become a regular rendezvous for the young – galling if you have spent a fortune on one of the beautiful Maids of Honour houses which were put up at the command of George I for the ladies of the court in attendance on the Prince of Wales.

After years of argument the prime riverside area running from the bridge (the oldest of all Thames bridges) to Mallard's restaurant and wine bar is finally being developed. The design is by Quinlan Terry and is generally regarded as 'safe' – better than some of the mindless office blocks which have gone up elsewhere in town – but also lacking in imagination and risk.

RICHMOND HILL

'...the ice rink...'

It epitomises a key Richmond trait – extreme tastefulness. A lot of Richmond is terribly *House and Garden* and National Trust shoppe. There are still a number of interesting old antique shops in the alleys around the Green and some fascinating second-hand bookshops on the hill, but Richmond has recently proved a magnet for such chic chain stores as Hatchards, Next, Laura Ashley and The Body Shop. If you wished to be unkind, you would say that there is too much machine-tooled lavender bag about the place. Mercifully, there are still islands of individual excellence – an imaginative little pub theatre, the Orange Tree; an unusual co-operative restaurant, Mrs Beaton's in the Twenty-first Century and Lichfield's, a modern, faintly antiseptic restaurant which consistently scores the highest marks in all the guides.

The swimming pool boasts the biggest indoor flume in Europe; the ice rink traditionally trains Olympic skaters; London Welsh, London Scottish, nearby Harlequins, Rosslyn Park and Richmond themselves make it easily the best place for rugger enthusiasts outside South Wales. The communications are excellent – a few minutes to the M3, lots of buses and three completely separate railway lines – the District Line tube, British Rail to Waterloo (under fifteen minutes with luck), which connects with places like Windsor and Reading in the other direction, and the North London Link which takes you through Hampstead and Islington right round to dockland.

No wonder that residents are inclined to be sniffy about their luck. Property prices have risen indecently. It's easily £500,000 for places on the Green, the Hill or up on Fife Road, where the Duke of Fife once had an estate complete with a Real Tennis court and a private cycling track. The most prominent local celebrity is Bamber Gascoigne who lives in one of the thin houses in St Helena Terrace overlooking the river. He features regularly in the Dimbleby-owned local paper, planting trees and chairing quizzes. Other celebrities such as the Attenborough brothers (David between hill and park, Dicky on the Green) tend to keep a lower profile.

Richmond was, with Kew, the undoing of T.S. Eliot. 'By Richmond I raised my knees/Supine on the floor of a narrow canoe.' Another literary association to put alongside 'The Lass of Richmond Hill', and one more indicator of a certain elegant excellence which is what Richmond likes to think it has. It is twinned with three foreign places – Richmond in Virginia, Fontainebleau and Konstanz. That tells you volumes about what Richmond-upon-Thames thinks of itself. And, to be fair, what others think of it.

A DAY AT THE TOWER

What does the Tower mean to those who visit it now?

After Charles II cleaned it up and drained the festering moat, the building with its evil silhouette set up to govern and subject a fractious capital since the first wood-and-earth tower of William the Conqueror, to house the mint and be the last fortified recourse of a monarch, became a popular site for outings. The menagerie, which in Elizabethan times had three lionesses, a tiger, a lynx and a wolf, was one attraction for the populace. Superstitious women stuck pins into the vast codpiece of Henry VIII's armour, hoping for a sympathetic magic to induce conception. He was the wrong man, I fear – his young son died of inherited syphilis and poisonous medicine that made his hair and nails fall out. Indeed, the suffering of those imprisoned from the king's ulcerated petulance almost surpassed that of his medieval predecessors. His wives, friends, advisers and enemies suffered mutually. One Tower guard claimed to have been chased at night by old Hal's bloody and floating head.

There is little that is pleasant in the Tower's long and functional history. People come for that reason alone. The sensibilities which drew the middle classes from Marylebone to Tyburn, to take cocoa overlooking the morning execution at eight, and to thrill to the highwayman who danced with his victims on Hampstead Heath now dancing partnerless, have little left the pysche.

Autocracy has a vivid handmaiden in torture. Argentinian juntas may still design chambers specially for the torture of pregnant women. However state-of-the-art the Tower was, we can only guess. Much of the pressure came from cold and deprivation, and serious neglect of the health of prisoners – such as Raleigh, and Bishop Fisher, who was so weakened by his experience that he had to be carried to the block. Treatment often depended on the caprice of the governor, who was frequently in the pay of private citizens. Sir Thomas Overbury was poisoned by just such a connection, though he had the constitution of Rasputin. His partridge was smeared with *lapis costitus*, his wine adulterated with mercury sublimate. Pepper was doctored with cantharides, salt with red and white arsenic. Great spiders, aqua fortis and lunar caustic were all introduced into his diet.

Few might resist the lively embrace of the Duke of Exeter's daughter (or the rack). A similar 'offspring' of the Duke of Skevington cramped prisoners in a cage till blood oozed from ears and eyes. There was the strappado, as well as pilliwinks, pyncbankis, caschielaws and bilboes to crack open ankles. There were those who had their jaws tightened with the brakes. Clever use was made of weights, brands, points and water treatment. The torture chamber was situated in the base of the White Tower, which in 1278 examined 600 Jews interned for 'coin-clipping' who were held in a small room above. A third of them were executed. No hint of this place now remains. Of the Little Princes found near the garderobes beside St John's Chapel, there are photographs and two exhumations. Of the thousand nameless victims whose shallow burials crowd the Tower precincts, a portion of them rest in metal boxes in the crypt of St Peter ad Vincula. A Yeoman Warder took me down there to see them. They are the result of an extensive sifting of the topsoil in recent years. Every rose tree that was planted revealed a mutilated skull or a twisted neck. Even now, only official authorisation can allow people to dig, for whatever reason. This is to minimise the bother of calling the police when human remains turn up. So much for the niceties of foul play! Standing in that chapel crypt one evening, amidst whitewash and inscriptions, was an experience that seemed frighteningly contemporary and familiar. Here were the graves of Hitler, the stadium of Chile, the rice fields of Korea, the latrines of Uganda. Is it likely that they will ever receive the same affection that we feel for the

Tower as a 'National Treasure' (*Reader's Digest*)? Amongst the bones lay the anonymous clutter of Thomas More. Upstairs lay Anne Boleyn, severed from life by a swordsman from St Omer, and bundled into a rough arrow chest.

The Tower's superannuated role is a peaceful one. Now, like Edinburgh Castle, it is the doting grandfather. Its status diminished, it is no longer a palace, the royal quarters ripped out by Cromwell, its bell-hung crown of Alfred the Great sold to an unknown speculator.

Yet I fancied that the ravens, standing on the green, stooped to hear the scratch of unsettled bones, and that the numerous trees planted thereabouts – if the haunted poets speak true – were never more crowded with the constituent parts of individual dissolution, waving their uneasy limbs. I never hold to the notion of ghosts seeking a consecrated grave, exchanging one damp nook for another.

Menagerie, Royal Observatory, Mint, place of Public Records, and the Crown Jewels; the Tower has been all these things – and its original purpose played down. Our ancestors would have recognised it as an enemy to freedom. When it was expanded with new buildings, feelings ran high in the capital. New work around Traitors' Gate caused the avenging spirit of Thomas à Becket to blast the battlements down with his crosier; indeed, a minor earthquake did happen at the time. That gate in particular was seen as the maw of the Tower. The well-educated Princess Elizabeth must have been quick to notice the classical connotations as the tide drifted her into the dark river-gate of the place where suspicion alone was enough to cause a death. She would appreciate that the weight of precedence didn't hold out much hope: she sat in the rain and wept by the riverside. She had a mournful comforter in that Tudor river. It was ever present to the prisoners, infecting their clammy cells with damp and fever, feeding the decayed moat with fumes. Its fog still rises to this day, and covers the iron bars and cold walls with a dew. Prisoners had to find other comforts in their cells. For Henry VI, it was his sparrow and breviary. Raleigh had his negroes and his laboratory, and Lady Hertford, monkeys, babies and carpets.

For a building popularised by torture, time and other diligent authorities have left little 'matter' behind them. It trades on, and yet overlooks, its reputation. The original torture chamber has disappeared. Few of its engines were kept for the curious. The endless tramp of visitors strung out in perpetual queues move something like a circulatory system in a dead beast populated with ravens and decorated armour. Step by step, they nudge through history in a continuous process of erasure. A block is on display, chock-marked. Practice? Nothing is said on the matter, and no one knows whether a wet finger drawn across its wooden nape would turn up the tastes of iron. The chambers of application so vividly described by Gerard, rush-lit, full of science, are filled with florets of muskets and quiet drums, like the entrance to a Tudor country house.

The truth is that from the Restoration onwards, monarchs preferred to distance themselves from the grisly utilitarianism of their power. James II was the last to indulge in the medieval pageantry of a coronation procession from the Tower, but up to George III monarchs had to spend the eve of their coronation there. If the present Prince of Wales were to revive the custom, he would probably have more opportunities for psychical research than anywhere else in the kingdom.

In 1840, Wellington defined its 'Waterloo Barracks' role (nothing escaped being named after his victory). The Victorians cleaned up the menagerie, and the last dingy lions were put under the care of a proper zoologist, who for the first time didn't feed them on brigands, thereby improving their health enormously. Its modern role of showcase and bank vault became clear. The Yeoman Warders, the order of personal bodyguards instigated by Henry VII, were encouraged to strut around and show off. It swiftly returned to the role of military base in war. A large contingent of regular soldiers still guards the Crown Jewels.

The Jewels merit a brief word. I have only ever once

bothered to queue up and look at them. A man named Colonel
Blood came closest to stealing them, and his cheek and daring
so impressed Charles II that the King gave him a pension.
Now they rest in modern conditions, in a large Chubb safe.
Sumptuous, mineral-encrusted signals of regality wink behind
steel-strengthened glass. Most of the major stones have a
hideous lineage; sapphires ripped from graves rest in a Maltese
Cross. The uncut ruby of the Black Prince, stolen from a
murdered king of Grenada, is there too. The Koh-hi-Nor
remains unparalleled among the loot of supernatural pillage.

I once visited the Bloody Tower at night, when it was lit
only by a hand-torch. It was on the invitation of a Yeoman
Warder, with whom I had had correspondence, at the age of
thirteen, about the Tower ghosts. I remember most the ghastly
light of the security neon glancing through the trees. The night
was warm and windy, so the shadows moved continually. In
my mind's eye I saw the hunchback king hovering over the
ivory casques of the Little Princes. On the narrow staircase
which led to their room I fancied I saw their discarnate faces,
shimmering like sad mirrors in their own poor glow. The
warder pointed to where the cutpurses had entered the Garden
Tower – as it was then known – from Raleigh's Walk (he was
to walk there later, and it is now named after him). They had
peered through a crack in a blocked-up window and crept in
to suffocate the crown princes under pathetic circumstances.

And indeed it was an eerie jaunt through the Tower in
the darkness, where shrouded lamps glanced off cobbled
streets, and tall shadows rose up the towering walls. The
Yeoman would stop to make particular the actual spot where
a ghost had appeared. I expected all manner of friends to
pour forth from a cracked paving-stone, or an indistinct
doorway.

> All my food is but vain hope of gain
> The day is past and yet I saw no sun
> And now I live and now my life is done.
>
> *Tichborne in the Tower*

Poets writing elegies before their deaths, or Raleigh visited by the Prince of Wales whilst working on his *History of the World*, leave us an elegant residue of a brutal place.

Pepys and even a king of France were one-time visitors to the cells, but none of these more famous guests suffered the same brutal ending as Monmouth, decapitated with a penknife, or received the torture of Guy Fawkes from the man Raleigh referred to as 'that beast Waad'. Some escaped, as Gerard did, down a rope, despite his mashed and blackened hands, to where some centuries earlier a polar bear, gift of the king of Norway, fished in the Thames. Mostly, the Tower was a place of anonymity. Very little is known of what happened there.

The elegies of Tichborne, Harington, and the poems of the imprisoned Orleans, are some of the few records we have. I had thought those millions of tourists scrubbed away the passages and chambers, ornate and self-decayed, and enacted a general amnesia in their visiting of kiosks and eating of cornettos. Would they stop when once a year Eton and Kings left lilies and sweet white roses in that place where their king-founder was murdered in prayer?

There are plenty of modern sites to take up the cause and break bones for the prevailing order. I am sure all modern torture in England is discreet and electronic. Memory is not attached to a place — neither is the cruel — and any spirit which lingers with a personal grudge does so in the cowl of its own dim hell.

SCHOOLS

Schools are a big dinner-party topic in London. The dinner-partying classes agonise over them as never before.

'Rowena's doing her A's at the new tertiary college. It's got a very good reputation.'

'Fiona's at Godolphin. She was fine at primary but honestly the choice at secondary is non-existent. Tony Benn's got no discipline whatever and St Frances Morrell's A-level results are appalling, so we had to go private.'

'Of course the Haughies are all right. They're Catholics.'

'Yes, it's different for the Catholics. Piers was down for Westminster which is Gyles' old school. Would you believe, they wouldn't take him? So we've sent him to Milton Abbey. They turn out an awfully nice sort of boy.'

'You know the Smith girl got pregnant. They blame it on the ILEA sex-education classes.'

'Thank God for Sarah's mother.'

The problems underlying this sort of conversation are complex and manifold. Among them are:

— Some dinner-party people feel guilty about paying for their children's education

— Some dinner-party people are very snobbish and not very well off

— Very few DPP are very well off and unsnobbish

— There are a number of rather good state primary schools but very few good secondaries

— Most of these are Roman Catholic although Cardinal Hume is doing his best to change this by destroying their sixth forms. Luckily the biggest and best of the Roman Catholic Schools — the London Oratory — is able to resist because the trustees are the fathers from the Brompton Oratory and they

'Schools are a big dinner-party topic in London.'

put the future of their school above the whim of the local bishop

– There is no fee-paying school in London for stupid people

– There is no really fashionable fee-paying school in London, except possibly for Westminster which is not half as smart as it thinks it is even though its setting, immediately behind Westminster Abbey, is very pretty

– The DPP, who used to think a chap could get by with a cut-glass accent, plausible manner and old school tie, have become belatedly convinced that everyone now needs qualifications. Suddenly *any* university is better than none.

None of this is of much interest to people who don't go to dinner parties or have school-age children. It is not even of much interest to school-age children, who tend to go wherever they are sent and grumble in a resigned but essentially cheerful manner, just like their grandparents when Jerry bombed them out of house and home during the blitz. Very British.

For the rest London schools loom surprisingly small. The most famous are either tucked away like Westminster which lurks almost invisible behind the Abbey or in new custom-built premises on the fringe, like St Paul's which looks like a modern computer factory – all prefabricated slabs on acres of playing field just south of Hammersmith bridge. London school-children are only visible in the early morning or middle of the afternoon when they clog the public transport system, hitting each other with decrepit shoulder bags, hurling insults at each other, smoking out of the corners of their mouths, chewing gum and swearing horribly. On Saturdays they can be found sitting spottily at the check-out counters of the capital's supermarkets.

Thanks to the progressive tendencies of the Inner London Education Authority, organised games are virtually unknown any longer. ILEA seems to think such things a threat to everything they hold most dear, unable to see, apparently, that in their own countries West Indians, Indians, and Pakistanis are passionate about cricket and can beat the daylights out of most pinko-Saxon teams from Britain. But if ever there was a chance for London's indigenous blacks to assert themselves, it could be through a hot school cricket league and ILEA is too bigoted and stupid to see this.

If you believe their critics, a similarly sandal-and-nut-cutlet attitude has permeated the academic curriculum as well so that all that happens behind those crumbling Victorian blood and bandage façades which dot London is peace studies, gay and lesbian studies and 101 interesting ways with plasticine with special application to the political situation in Namibia.

In fact middle-class parent power, not to mention a strong traditionalist element among many London teachers, has meant that some London state schools are more academically competitive than ever. Several primary schools in middle-class areas such as Putney, Dulwich, Hampstead and Highgate have almost eclipsed the traditional private preparatory school in providing fodder for fee-paying secondary schools. And some of the new tertiary and sixth-form colleges – Richmond for example – have set a spanking academic pace. They are also a lot more attractive to seventeen-year-old Fionas and Piers than some antideluvian convent in Shropshire or dim boarding school in a small country town dead from the neck up. And as the DPP are aware the churches, particularly the Roman Catholic Church, still preside over a free education where the most successful aspire to Oxford and Cambridge, where the choir sings in the cathedral and the XI still plays in long white trousers.

There are other odd centres of excellence. The French Lycée gets good reports and there are any number of other national schools, even one for the Welsh. For the unconventional, King Alfred's, Hampstead, is said to provide 'an engagingly eccentric and mature environment'. And for what one head-master describes as 'those awkward gaps in the educational process' you could not do better than Mander, Portman and Woodward – a crammer's (they would prefer 'tutorial college') in Kensington.

Generally speaking, though, London education is not what

one should expect of a great capital city, particularly at secondary level. Certainly it comes nowhere near matching the standards of its often brilliant collegiate University with its numerous centres of international excellence.

An expert recommends:

	Boys	Girls
Fashionable, clever and rich	Westminster	St Paul's
Clever, not so rich	St Paul's	North London Collegiate
Clever, poor	William Ellis	Camden School for Girls
Not so clever, rich	Boarding school	Frances Holland
Not so clever, nor so rich	Emanuel	Putney High School

PRISONS

'To Fortune – a much maligned lady.' If the result of the toast is the same as it was for Paul Pennyfeather, then you are going to need help. This is especially so if the magistrate lacks understanding or mercy and refuses to grant you bail, for you will be taken to Brixton Prison on remand.

This hostelry is no longer – as described by Mayhew in 1850 – 'situate in one of the most open and salubrious spots in the southern suburbs of London.' Indeed life inside is grim, boring and thoroughly overcrowded. The cuisine is very limited and tends to be warmed up an infinite amount of times. You are not encouraged to enquire for a sightseeing tour of the route followed by Denis Tuite and his friends when they escaped from the maximum-security confines of the prison. There is plenty of time to think about your case: over twenty-three hours a day in your cell and opportunity enough to discuss it with the other two who share it. Try not to have any stomach trouble. Indeed try not to be ill at any time as medicine and the doctors are rough and ready. In all, the atmosphere is such that you should press your brief to redouble his efforts to acquire bail.

As for your trial, remember there is always a chance. You would be well advised to find out which courts have a good record of acquittals. The rule of thumb is that the Old Bailey is not a particularly good bet but has produced spectacularly eccentric results. St Alban's tends to vote guilty with precision but the Snaresbrook juries are always worth a try.

If you are convicted, you should give up smoking there and then. There will always be opportunities for acquiring drugs but these are expensive. Locally made hooch will be available – fire extinguishers make the best stills – but is not recommended. The hangover is diabolical if you survive that long.

With no previous convictions you will go, if sentenced, to Wormwood Scrubs in west London, now more security-conscious than in the days when the double agent George Blake was able to walk out when no one was looking. It has changed very little since its governor John McCarthy described it as 'a penal dustbin' in 1981. He resigned in despair a year later. Its four vast halls are surrounded by barbed wire and it resembles nothing so much as a stultifying cage. Built over a hundred years ago by forced labour in unhealthy marshland it echoes nowadays to constant banging and crashing and is in a permanent fog of builders' dust as vain efforts are made to hold the thing together and prevent it from subsiding into the boggy ground below.

If you are in need of the consolations of religion, you will be able to visit the chapel, an enormous Victorian Romanesque monstrosity which is widely regarded as the cathedral of the prison service. It was due to be knocked down but was saved by the dramatic last-minute intervention of Willie Whitelaw when he was Home Secretary. There is no commemorative plaque.

There is one gallows in full working order – just in case! It is at Wandsworth Prison. This is a place to avoid if possible, preferably by getting yourself sent to an open prison in the shires where you will meet a higher class of prisoner (swindlers, embezzlers, conmen, etc.) and can play cricket and football against local teams. Wandsworth has a gloomy, threatening atmosphere built into its whole fabric. The staff's oppressive bad manners and air of aggrieved machismo is seemingly handed down from generation to generation. It is overcrowded and stultifying. Do not ask how Ronald Biggs escaped from here. Your interest will be misinterpreted. Above all, do be careful to whom you talk in the food queue. Your natural good manners will be misinterpreted by the rival gang and you may undergo oversharp persuasion to reappear 'neutral'.

If your sentence is short, you may well be sent to Pentonville, just north of King's Cross. This houses the failed criminals

'Prisoners and staff easily lose their way . . .'

who are on the 'roundabout' – no sooner out than in again. Pathetic flea-ridden drunks and social incompetents overfill a building which was once *the* model prison. Recent attempts at refurbishing have made it, curiously, yet more shabby and you will search in vain for the return to integral sanitation with which every cell was equipped in 1840. In fact the last piece of treasured cast-iron piping, which represents this attempt by the Victorians at civilised imprisonment is now exhibited, but not, alas, for use. The uniformed staff who claim to run Pentonville are prickly and quick to take offence so you need to be obsequious in your dealings with authority.

Up the road, 'the castellated grandeur of the city prison at Holloway' alas exists no longer. With the true vandalism that only the gleaming reformer can produce it was knocked down just over ten years ago to be replaced by the genuine disaster of the new Holloway. Here unfortunate women of all kinds and conditions are housed in modern, well-intentioned, very expensive squalor. It takes real genius to design such an appalling building. The confusion of benign intentions and penal reality can be seen with the twisting 'crinkle-crankle' external wall – neither use nor ornament. Inside, its narrow passages and tiny rooms are maze-like. Prisoners and staff easily lose their way and become disorientated. Few grasp where they are except inside, in a moody, unhappy claustrophobic atmosphere. This seemingly affects everyone who lives and works in Holloway. Clearly, it should be blown up.

In short there is little to recommend in London's prisons. Overcrowded, shabby and falling to pieces; try to get bail and a suspended sentence.

CLUBS

Cockroaches, Peter de Savary, pumping iron, briefcases, Carmen Callil and others of her sex have reared their heads. The old St James's, the Senior (United Service), Bath, and the tacky Junior Carlton have bitten the dust, while the Guards, and the United University are among those who have had to merge with other clubs which is much the same thing. Bernard Levin, Lord Weinstock, the Honourable Rocco Forte and Mark Thatcher have suffered the proverbial sheep-shit. These are a few of the happenings, or non-happenings, which have disturbed the features of clubland since the *New London Spy* was published in 1966.

The cockroaches were spotted in various club kitchens, where they had doubtless bred happily for generations without harming the nursery food, by a bureaucrat with an apparent grudge against clubland. In the words of Walter Annenberg, a familiar figure in St James's in the early 1970s, 'an element of refurbishment' — a phrase he invented for England — became the urgent alternative to closure at such clubs as Brooks's and the Travellers'. The tarting up of the latter club *à la* Trusthouse Forte raised the eyebrows of the architectural historians among the membership which the committee did not see fit to consult.

Mr Annenberg himself is a member of the oppressively grand White's at the top of St James's which is to clubs what Eton is to public schools – the *nonpareil*. When a new member asked old Wheeler, the now-retired barman, if the bar was open, he received the reply: 'Bless my soul, sir, it has been open for 200 years.'

White's, where the Prince of Wales had a bachelor dinner before his wedding, has the longest waiting list of any club except for the MCC which is not quite the same thing. (It is now reckoned to be about ten years.) However, being a rich establishment buoyed up by investments, the subscription and the scrumptious food is comparatively cheap once you get in. Getting in is the problem, as Rocco Forte and his proposer Lord Charles Spencer-Churchill (an employee of the hoteliers) discovered. This embarrassing incident was regarded as a low point in a place where 'happenings' of the sort featuring the lamented Randolph Churchill, Ed Stanley, Evelyn Waugh, Sir Iain Moncreiffe of that Ilk and other heroes of yesteryear, are increasingly rare. Evelyn's son, Auberon, has pointed out that White's has become full of big-bottomed businessmen. Were it not now defamatory to comment on the size of people's buttocks, no bottom could be said to be bigger at White's than that of the carnationed Lord Michael Pratt, a comforting example of the clubman of the old school, though barely forty.

Appropriately enough, Lord Michael is also a member of Pratt's (no relation), surely the most beguiling 'nightclub' in London. The cosily ramshackle basement dining-room off St James's only holds about a dozen, any of whom are liable to range from backwoods peers to Malcolm Muggeridge. Conversation is delightfully haphazard, but this is not perhaps the best place to try out the joke about selling old masters to acquire young mistresses. The club is owned by the Duke of Devonshire.

Whereas at Pratt's the staff all answer to the name of 'George' (so much simpler if one has drink taken), those at the Beefsteak are all called 'Charles'. If Pratt's is a dining club, the Beefsteak is essentially a lunch club. Unfortunately you have to sit next to the person whose signature is last in the book; this accounts for a certain amount of hovering. In an age of narrow-minded specialisation and careerism, club bores are a growth industry.

The Garrick, another 'clubbable' club in the vicinity of Covent Garden, has recently enjoyed a remarkable resurgence and is one of the few clubs, apart from White's, to have a lengthy waiting list. Noisy and rather hearty, the place always

'. . . White's has become full of big-bottomed businessmen.'

seems full of bearded publishers and loud-mouthed lawyers hoping to be taken for thespians. A show of upholding the club's theatrical traditions is made by the odd fat-cat performer like Donald Sinden or Derek Nimmo, but it is said that if Garrick himself were put up for election now he would be blackballed by the judges who did for poor Levin.

The Garrick, with its mass of pictures and stage memorabilia, seems to appeal more than most old-fashioned clubs to women, who are allowed into the distinctively reddish dining-room in the evening, but not for lunch. To combat this discrimination, a group of 'media' people including Carmen Callil, the formidable feminist publisher who began her career as a club waitress (at the 'satirical' Establishment, now defunct), have set up a new unisex club in Soho and called it Groucho's – thereby ruining a tolerable old joke of Mr Marx's. The direly decorated result reminds one of nothing so much as a Sydney singles' bar, full of researchers from *Wogan* and book-packagers staring self-consciously at one another over the kiwi fruit. Occasionally they are rewarded with the glimpse of the odd figure from 'public-iety' such as Tim ('Puffed') Rice.

Following a split-beaver model who posed across the club's leather armchairs for a girlie magazine, more respectably dressed businesswomen entered the nicotine-stained portals of the Reform in Pall Mall. The young fogeys of the Travellers' next door may have viewed such a development as deserving of such an unfortunately named establishment, but an unsympathetic committee of their own club (christened the 'Fellow-Travellers' at the time of the Blunt revelations) were soon also springing women upon them at unwonted times of the day. Monsignor Gilbey, however, continues to say mass in the old boot room.

Somehow, traditional clubland carries on. Brooks', which survived an IRA bomb and the blackballing of Arnie Weinstock, still resembles a duke's town house with the duke lying dead upstairs while below the doyen of the Alliance swigs claret like the butler he so resembles. Boodle's is still full of bibulous baronets and refugees from the City ('Not worth going back after lunch') watching the racing on television. This club's ladies' annexe has proved an astute commercial venture. The Turf, spruced up and sleek, acts as a convenient waiting room for White's. The Savile is a downmarket Garrick; the Eccentric is infested with Lord's Taverners plotting how to get on the Honours List; the Arts is full of chartered surveyors; the RAC engagingly anonymous, and the various military clubs become ever more colourless. The food at Buck's (rather too full of the Morley clan if not yet of the Thatcher dynasty) and the Athenaeum is still atrocious.

There is also a new clubland reflecting the ineffably vulgar mood of Thatcher's Britain. Its sybaritic citizens are not charmed by the escapist delights of shabby misanthropic and misogynist nineteenth-century gloom, the attempt to hold back the flood of business talk, nannyish scott or even the still incredibly cheap claret and bedrooms. Their desire for conspicuous consumption is gratified at establishments run by the likes of Mark Birley (of Annabel's fame), John ('Aspers') Aspinall and Peter de Savary, proprietor of the new St James's. A disturbing foretaste of the future could once be savoured – at a considerable price – in the basement of the New Piccadilly Hotel. There, the Gleneagles Club, which had a torture chamber complete with a 'leg extension machine', 'stomach isolator' and other instruments of health fascism, bragged nonsensically of 'the values of a traditional London club, with none of the restrictions imposed by such an institution'. An enquiry as to whether the membership was mixed brought the response: 'Oh no, we are dealing with a *very exclusive* clientele.'

HOTELS

'The best method the reader can use to avoid the insolence and ingratitude of these Mungril sort of Christians is . . . never to use any one House long . . . the vitiousness of the Age has occasion'd every parish to abound with such great numbers of the morose, mercenary, foul, fat-feeding, un-neighbourly cormorants.'

Ned Ward, *London Spy*, 1705

For 300 years the *Spy* has hated inns and their descendants, hotels. Such a view seems part of the English national character. He still despised hotels in the 1960s; it is so frightfully *bourgeois* to stay in one. If you came up to London and stayed in a hotel it meant you didn't have an Auntie Babs (aka the Duchess of Baubles) or a cousin, the Honourable Henry Hurrah (fifth cousin twice removed, your age, played together under the Christmas tree), who lived in town all year round. While the hipper seventies' *Spy* gave the decade-older *Spy* a reprimand for being so frumpy as to advise against having an overnight *affaire d'amour* in a hotel, he too whittered on, lamenting that London hoteliers had a hold of us by the delicate parts of our anatomy owing to a shortage of hotel rooms.

He was a wiseacre, but he was right. Guerrilla warfare was suggested as the most expedient method of convincing hotel personnel and owners that they were in the business for *him*, not themselves. He wasn't very happy about the way the troops were carrying out orders, either. He reminded us that we were just as frumpy as our by-this-time-old-age-pensioner of a secret serviceman for thinking hotels were solely for sleeping in. He accused us of not using hotel lounges or their lavatories, or even their bars and their restaurants, because of our funny old-fashioned notions that we should be paying before we took advantage of their facilities.

The bad news is this. Hotel proprietors still have a hold of us by the short-and-curlies; prices have gone from the ridiculous to the sublime, with not a room in town available for much under £50. These days there are multitudes of hotels, many in pathetically bad taste, all making an enormous profit. We will use a hotel lavatory only if desperate (the ones at the Park Lane are pretty nice, but who ever happens to be walking by there when struck?), and we know better than to be caught dead abusing our palates and purses at most hotel restaurants (except perhaps for the 'Menu Surprise' at the Dorchester). Sadly, it is still wise to bear in mind the timeless advice of my predecessor: 'It is essential, if coming to London, to grasp the fact that British hotels exist primarily for the convenience of those employed in them and, secondly, for the profits of the owners.'

The good news I admit the scene has improved somewhat. There has been response from hoteliers to the consumer's simple demand that he get something in return for the extortionate price he must pay for a hotel room in London. And almost everybody these days will confess that it's bliss to be pampered, anonymous and carefree with money (or pampered, anonymous, and giggling about not having to dip into the life savings for a weekend soirée) in a hotel that has more business sense than not to cater to your every whim. (The few aristocratic dinosaurs who remain unconvinced should be sent out to stay with the 7th Earl of Bradford's mother at Weston Park in Shropshire, even if they haven't been properly introduced. The Earl makes room for up to thirty *paying* guests.)

London's hotels fall nicely – with the ever-present non-conformist mucking up the outline – into three categories: Grand Hotels, Smaller Hotels with Character, and The Rest.

Some of the Grand Hotels were around when the great German traveller/lister Karl Baedeker – a fellow spy – came to London in the late nineteenth century: the Savoy, the

Berkeley (the old one was on the corner of Berkeley Street and Piccadilly), Brown's, Claridge's. They retain their elegance and dignity, their snooty employees and clientele, and recreate for the lucky imbiber the utter luxury of the Grand Tour. Once you arrive, it takes about three minutes to forget you haven't always lived this way and you are overcome with shame to have forgotten the monogrammed trunk with room for twenty-four pairs of evening slippers. These magnificent hotels are for the extremely wealthy, the honeymooners and those celebrating a whim.

Some of the Smaller Hotels with Character are just that; others are a fairly recent innovation, deserving of much applause and reflecting the above-mentioned modern man and woman's growing insistence on excellence – a sort of 'New Georgian' desire to sprinkle beauty, quality and good taste over everything on the plate. It is the high standards of the owners of these hotels, who take a personal interest in their creations, and their prices – not much more than £20 higher – that make The Rest seem so dire. Smaller Hotels with Character are for seasoned travellers who know better than to think that it's Belgium just because it's Tuesday.

The Rest the *Spy* will let you suffer on your own. These hotels are uniform in decor and price (and dreadful coffee), and are supremely indicative of what Hilary Rubinstein, editor of *The Hotel Guide*, pegs 'the industry's complacent resistance to self-improvement'. It makes precious little difference that they display small red, white and blue rectangular plaques or flowered circular ceramic ones (for goodness' sake, neither are to be confused with blue plaques), proclaiming registration with the English Tourist Board or membership of the British Hotels, Restaurants and Caterers' Association. These simply mean the hotel has registered and/or paid dues. You are still likely to sleep in a tiny room, between nylon sheets on a sagging bed, surrounded by veneered furniture which you can't see because the fifty-watt bulb in the one lamp has blown, and shower the next morning down the hall in a cubicle that produces three drops of lukewarm water in slow procession for three minutes. The *Spy* of 1705 knew about The Rest. He described with uncanny accuracy a room in a hotel in South Kensington that I'm sure I stayed in once: '. . . A room not much bigger than a hogshead, furnished with nothing but a little bedstead, and that of an easy height to fit in; we found . . . we had little likelihood of a resting place, but either forced to lie down like dogs, or lean like elephants . . .' The Rest are for The Rest and students with backpacks.

Grand Hotels

Brown's, Dover Street, W1

Wood-panelled, understated and dignified. Suites large and comfortable. Huge bathroom fixtures from another era, but plumbing commendable. If you don't happen to be staying here, have morning coffee in the lounge anyway: £1.20 for a little pot of that unchristian brew.

Claridge's, Brook Street, W1

If the landed gentry were reduced to putting someone up in a hotel in London, it would probably be this one. A *passé* but immortal place, full of tradition. Obsequious service. Jackets and ties handed out to gentlemen so they may walk through the lobby. Scored a huge triumph with a *Spy* of yesteryear for cool when, during a night-time fire, fleeing pyjamaed guests were welcomed with champagne in the lounge. Claridges simply doesn't change and for this most patrons heave a sigh of relief.

Connaught, Carlos Place, W1

Impeccable in every way, and probably the most exclusive grand hotel in London. Good wine list in the restaurant; freezing cocktails. Gentlemen are expected to wear a jacket and tie. Jan Morris is thinking of maintaining a permanent suite here 'when my boat comes in'. Better get your bid in quickly.

Dorchester, Park Lane, W1

Luxurious and international. Don't bother to take your car, unless it's at least two city blocks long and would look nice parked in front with all the rest. Irretrievably 1930s inside and out. Caters to every whim, because it has to. (A whole roast sheep was once served to a sheikh and his followers sitting on the floor.) At the time of writing, owned by the Sultan of Brunei but don't take my word for it. You could be sleeping in a bed once slept in by (or just maybe, sleeping in it this very moment) King Hussein, Liz Taylor, or Gregory Peck.

Meridian Piccadilly, Piccadilly, W1

Renovations inside Richard Norman Shaw's grand, conceited building look top class and extravagant, bordering on flash. (The *Spy* forgot it was there. It's been under scaffolding for years.) Boasts Italian marble bathrooms, a tremendous sports facility called (a little pretentiously) the Champneys Club, and a glass-enclosed terrace restaurant. Keep fingers crossed that food and service continue to be top class too.

Ritz, Piccadilly, W1

For tourists. Rich, glamorous tourists. But stay here anyway and drink champagne. It's a dream come true. Just don't have tea here. Have tea at Brown's.

Savoy, Strand, WC2

The pink and green suites overlooking the Thames are worth every bit of the couple of hundred more that they will cost you than the bedrooms across the hall, which are just ordinary top-class opulence. Spend your honeymoon in one of these gems, and the discreet staff will push the twin beds together, cover them with one big sheet and you will have a playground bigger than your sitting room at home. Walk hand in hand over the warm tiles in the bathroom to the swimming pool that they call a bathtub. Chase one another through both walk-in closets. Order orange juice for breakfast and marvel at where the waiter got all that crushed ice. Lord Forte, eat your heart out.

Smaller Hotels With Character

Basil Street Hotel, 8 Basil Street, SW3

Actually just as big as the Connaught but belongs in this category because it is substantially less expensive. Quiet and highly traditional, reputed to have good, friendly service. (Another reason for listing it here. Staff members at the Grand Hotels would be highly insulted if you said to them, 'Gosh, you're friendly.') You still must ask for an *en suite* bath. *Painfully* close to Harrods.

Durrants Hotel, George Street, W1

One of those late eighteenth-century terraces, with the most magnificent Robert Adamesque overdoor. Mock-Brown's entrance hall (or lack thereof). Patronised by art historians from all over the western world, mostly of the 'art is for art historians' type (although American museum directors stay at the Westbury on New Bond Street). Wouldn't you know, the Wallace Collection is right around the corner. I admit Durrants has as many rooms as the Connaught too, but this hotel is jolly good value for money.

L'Hotel, 28 Basil Street, SW3

So lovely it's almost twee. Done in pretty French rustic style, soft all over. Very modern, with every convenience except a lounge. I've heard the continental breakfast served in your room is worth the whole bill. Also painfully close to Harrods.

Number 16, 16 Sumner Place, SW7

This one is a Victorian building (actually, four Victorian buildings, all in a row). No sign on the door. Although now owned by Granfel, the perfect example of an elegant, small hotel in which the founder owner had taken a personal interest. Outdoor garden available for guests when it's warm. Jan Morris may dream about the Connaught, but she stays here. If Number 16 is fully booked, go across the street to the Alexander, 9 Sumner Place.

Portobello Hotel, 22 Stanley Gardens, W11

Almost eccentric enough to be in a category of its own. You want to compare it with New York's Chelsea Hotel, but you know you can't. The Portobello Hotel may have an avant-garde personality, but at least it's *nice*. Some of the rooms are called cabins – yes, very small, but ask for a big room and you'll get one if they're not all booked. The restaurant is open twenty-four hours. Portobello Market (antiques, food, junk) on Saturdays.

Wilbraham Hotel, 1 Wilbraham Place, SW1

No one bothered to tear down the original staircases, archways and woodwork when they converted this genteel, atmospheric place from three private houses into a hotel. It is alleged that you can almost certainly always get a room here after 6 pm or so. Reasonably priced.

CHURCHES

The vast suburban churches
Together we have found:
The ones which smelt of gaslight
The ones in incense drown'd;
I'll use them now for praying in
And not for looking round.
Collected Poems, Murray (Publishers) Ltd

So runs the second verse of Sir John Betjeman's poem, 'The Cockney Amorist'. Since Betjeman wrote his essay on London Churches in the first *Spy*, much has changed and the Londoner today will find it much more difficult both to look round and to pray in churches. This is not because conditions have reverted to those of the nineteenth century when, according to George Gilbert Scott junior – architect of two lost London churches – a man was stopped from saying his prayers in Westminster Abbey by a verger: 'No praying allowed here by order of the Dean and Chapter – hours of divine service 10 and 4'. It is just that so many more churches are closed except on Sunday mornings and it is often difficult to find the key. This is because of vandalism: a real danger. And this does not only mean the theft of candlesticks and the other examples of ecclesiastical craftsmanship which are all part of the interest of visiting churches. It can also mean arson. St Matthew's, Westminster, and Barnes Parish Church were both destroyed by mad arsonists in the 1970s. (Both, encouragingly, have since been interestingly rebuilt; but now, in 1987, St Peter's Eaton Square has been gutted.)

Sadly, much vandalism is also committed by the Church of England itself. The reordering of churches and the installation of free-standing 'forward' altars has led to the spoiling of many church interiors. It can be done well – visit

St Anne's, Hoxton, to see how (if it has not been spoilt since 1985) – but usually the new woodwork is obtrusive and the obligatory mustard-yellow or pale-green carpeting always looks ghastly. Much worse, of course, is the closure and demolition of churches. Many churches have been closed in the Diocese of London since 1969, including several recommended by Betjeman; others are threatened. The Church of England is in retreat and a mood of defeatism, masquerading as financial realism, pervades the clergy. Church buildings are regarded as so much ecclesiastical 'plant', which is often surplus to requirements, and so great buildings, upon which love, care and sacrifice has been devoted, which tell us so much about the character and aspirations of Londoners of the past, are wilfully closed and destroyed, regardless of the feelings of people who live locally. For, whatever the Church Commissioners may think, churches are seen as symbols of faith as well as landmarks; the significance of their closure is not lost on ordinary people, who usually feel a great sense of loss when their parish church goes.

Churches are monuments. They are seen as monuments, both by Londoners and by visitors. They are both symbols of our Christian past and works of architecture of the greatest interest. Nobody interested in the topography and architecture of London can ignore the churches. They include some of the finest buildings of their times and their interiors almost always justify the effort of securing the key at the vicarage or the churchwarden's house. And, if you are interested as well in what goes on in them – in church-going, in liturgy, in the visual expressions of different types of worship, then the rewards of church crawling are even greater. They are the stuff of life and of culture.

The interest of London's churches is unlike that of many other European cities, for the best date from the seventeenth, eighteenth, nineteenth and even the twentieth centuries – the centuries following the introduction of Italian Renaissance architecture into England, including the period of the great, creative reaction of the Gothic Revival which looked back to

the Middle Ages for inspiration. Of real medieval buildings, there are few of any real significance. Westminster Abbey, of course, is in a class of its own and best seen when it is open on a winter's evening, free of tourists and admission charges; then the great royal tombs are awesome in the gloom. Otherwise there are just the City churches which escaped the Great Fire – haphazard medieval relics on the eastern fringes of the City – and the Temple Church which, after restoration and reconstruction, is virtually all nineteenth- and twentieth-century.

There are, however, two medieval churches which are of real interest. One is St Bartholomew-the-Great by Smithfield Market, which is a fragment of the great Norman priory and hospital church which, after years of degradation, was well restored by Aston Webb in the 1890s. The other is St Etheldreda's in Ely Place, originally the chapel of the Bishop of Ely. His palace gave way to sober Georgian terraces, in the middle of which suddenly appears a church façade with beautiful tracery of the Decorated Gothic period. This chapel was sold in 1871 by the Welsh Episcopalians and bought by Roman Catholics, so this is a rare case of a medieval church returning to the faith for which it was built. After war damage, good stained glass was installed by Joseph Nuttgens.

The Renaissance came to London with Inigo Jones, who left us the Chapel Royal by St James' Palace and St Paul's, Covent Garden, with its great Tuscan portico dominating the piazza. But it is the churches of Wren, the happy product of the catastrophe of 1666, which show Classicism adapted to English conditions. St Paul's Cathedral, of course, is an austere, awe-inspiring patriotic marvel which can be difficult to enjoy, thanks to the tourists, the moneychangers' tables, hotel-style revolving glass doors, hideous seats and the other indignities to which this great building has been subjected in recent years.

More rewarding, because so much more intimate and modest, are the City churches. Often simple brick buildings, each different in plan, raised on the irregular foundations of the churches destroyed in the Great Fire, they were once conspicuous for the imaginative variety of their steeples which gave London a skyline that was actually admired by foreign visitors. Wren's City churches are rightly regarded as a great achievement and one of our national treasures. Sadly, however, the truth is that the skyline has gone, submerged by taller buildings, and that few of the churches look today as they did in Wren's time. Many have been demolished or mutilated internally by Victorians who despised the style of Wren. Others were bombed and have been rebuilt in a presumptuous or insensitive manner. Some of the most famous are just not worth seeing. The ones that are, which preserve the musty atmosphere and white-plastered walls with elaborately carved, dark woodwork, must be sought out down the surviving narrow streets of the old City. They include St Margaret's, Lothbury; St Martin's, Ludgate; that humble marvel with its painted dome, St Mary Abchurch; St Magnus the Martyr by London Bridge, enlivened by sympathetic Anglo-Catholic Baroque additions in the 1920s; and St Mary at Hill in Lovat Lane. This last still preserves its high box-pews and conveys an authentic impression of Wren's time despite its pretty early-Victorian plaster ceiling. It is sad that St Stephen's, Walbrook, Wren's famous try-out for the dome of St Paul's, should now have its subtle geometry and authentic character destroyed by a preposterous central circular altar made by Henry Moore and given by Mr Peter Palumbo, the property developer, who lives next door.

Wren inaugurated a most creative period in English architecture which expressed itself as much in churches as in country houses. The best of these are in London, thanks to Queen Anne's so-called Fifty New Churches Act of 1711, which gave the capital not fifty but twelve great monumental buildings of Portland stone to proclaim the supremacy of the Church of England over dissenters and heretics. This campaign of building allowed the pupils and successors of

Wren to design works which are of European significance, in that native development of classicism which historians have called the 'English Baroque'.

The most prominent of these is St Martin-in-the-Fields in the corner of Trafalgar Square, designed by James Gibbs, that smooth Scotsman who had to keep his Roman Catholicism well suppressed. Although trained in Rome – after giving up thoughts of the priesthood – Gibbs here committed a great solecism which, ironically, proved extraordinarily successful. He combined a portico with a steeple by having the latter rising illogically and unprecedentedly out of the roof of the former. That this now seems quite natural is partly because there are versions of the design all over the world – in America, in India, in Australia. This is due to the fact that clever, ambitious Gibbs published the design in his *Book of Architecture*. The prototype of this familiar Anglican archetype is impressive for its noble deep Corinthian portico and for its interior with its richly modelled plaster ceiling and its original box-pews and galleries below.

Gibbs also designed St Mary-le-Strand, which is more Roman and less solecistic. That fashionable Mayfair church, St George's, Hanover Square, designed by John James, is another church of the same type and period, as is St Giles-in-the-Fields, by Flitcroft, and St George's, Bloomsbury, by Hawksmoor, with its noble portico and weird steeple topped by a statue of Queen Anne's successor, George I. But for the best of the Fifty New Churches and for some of the most moving and sublime buildings in London, the church crawler must go east and penetrate some of the poorest – but far from uninteresting – parts of the capital. Near Deptford Station, on London's oldest railway, proudly stands St Paul's Church, a great pile of Portland stone designed by Thomas Archer, a real baroque architect who had trained in Rome. This great monument, with its circular steeple rising logically above a semi-circular portico defies modern Anglican wisdom by being a living symbol of faith as well as of history in a much-deprived area. The services in St Paul's and its parish life, as well as its architecture, are inspiring and demonstrate that fine buildings and a living, thriving Christian community are not incompatible.

Greatest of all are the Stepney churches of Wren's great pupil, Nicholas Hawksmoor. These three remarkable buildings have long obsessed architects and anyone else with a taste for the strange and the monumental, but it is important to stress that they are not the sinister, diabolical creations of the eponymous villain in Peter Ackroyd's clever, mischievous novel. They are, rather, the products of an unusual and inventive mind, obsessed with the antique, with – unusually – the Gothic and with the sublime. Furthest out is St Anne's, Limehouse, in what was once Chinatown. It remains a proud, powerful symbol in an area which is now being transformed by the redevelopment of Docklands. Then comes St George's-in-the-East, just off what used to be called the Ratcliffe Highway and in what was once one of the most desperate parts of London. In the 1850s, St George's was the scene of vile anti-Ritualist riots; more recently its great tower, of bold masses of stone, topped by a Gothic-looking lantern, overshadowed the riots outside Rupert Murdoch's Fortress Wapping. Its interior was blitzed and today a clever modern church, by Arthur Bailey, occupies part of the vast space within Hawksmoor's great walls. Last but not least comes Christ Church, Spitalfields, closest to the City but in a very different world. This, arguably Hawksmoor's greatest masterpiece, has been closed since the 1960s but, at last, is being carefully restored by the Friends of Christ Church, Spitalfields. In the summer, concerts are held in its gaunt, basilica-like interior. These are intended to generate interest in a building which, it is hoped, will become both a church again and a concert hall. The first glimpse of its vast west tower, with a spire above a triumphal arched belfry, itself above a portico in the shape of a Palladian window, rising above the bustle of Spitalfields Market (now doomed) and the squalor of this fascinating early-

Georgian quarter, is almost the most dramatic sight in all London.

After wonderful Hawksmoor, the churches of the rest of the eighteenth century are an anti-climax. There is the Grosvenor Chapel in South Audley Street, a simple brick building which is only really interesting because of the sumptuous twentieth-century internal improvements made by Comper. Similarly, John Plaw's little St Mary's, Paddington Green, is worth seeing because of the beautiful recreation of its late eighteenth-century character by Raymond Erith and Quinlan Terry which was carried out owing to the compensation derived from the construction of the Westway, which runs right next door. The most interesting Georgian church is no longer a church; that is, All Hallows, London Wall, built by George Dance junior – the master of Soane – whose austere, neoclassical interior is now used as a library by the Council for the Care of Churches.

Sir John Soane himself, the original, strange architect of the Bank of England, designed three London churches under the Church Building Act of 1818; the best of these is St Peter's, Liverpool Grove, off the Walworth Road in south London. This was the last occasion when state money would be devoted to church building – by a government fearful of the connection between atheism and revolution demonstrated by the French. The resulting Commissioners' Churches are to be found in all the inner-London suburbs and are often galleried brick boxes with a western steeple. In south London there are the so-called 'Waterloo Churches' dedicated to the Four Evangelists – St Matthew's, Brixton; St Mark's, Kennington; St Luke's, Norwood; and St John's, Waterloo Road – all fine neoclassical designs outside and all wrecked inside. A few were Gothic (it was cheaper – no stone required for porticoes). The best is St Luke's, Chelsea, built by James Savage. This has flying buttresses supporting the stone vault. There is a story that an early congregation once panicked and fled the building fearing that this unusual structure (for the time) was about to collapse.

By far the best church of the early nineteenth century is also the most sumptuous Greek Revival building in London other than the British Museum. This is the New Church of St Pancras on the corner of Euston Square (old Old St Pancras Church, possibly one of the oldest Christian sites in England, lies behind St Pancras Station, but it was so spoiled by restoration in the 1840s that it is now only really worth visiting to see the strange tomb of Sir John Soane in the churchyard). Designed by the Inwoods, father and son, the New Church is really St Martin-in-the-Fields translated into Greek, with no expense spared. The portico is Greek Ionic, the vestries have caryatids from the Erectheum and the steeple is a development of the Tower of the Winds. Inside there are galleries on iron columns, box-pews (cut down in size, alas) and sumptuous Greek-Revival furniture. The general effect is rich, dark and somehow rather secular. It is just the sort of building that Pugin and the forthcoming wave of moralising Gothicists would dismiss as 'Pagan' because it is classical and not in the 'true Christian style' – that is, Gothic.

Owing both to the proselytising of Pugin – who, with Barry, created the Palace of Westminster and who believed that architecture was inseparable from religion – and to a great revival within the Church of England after the Oxford Movement in the 1830s, the Gothic Revival became a most powerful force. It ended the classical tradition in church architecture which began with Jones, and covered London with new churches in a very different style. Because the best and brightest architects in the mid-Victorian years wanted to design churches, some remarkable and noble buildings were produced. Some of the Victorian churches of London are amongst the best there are. No longer easily despised, they can be seen as inspired expressions of fervent faith – like the medieval prototypes which initially inspired them.

Like all revivals, the Gothic Revival went through several distinct phases. The first, analogous to the Early Renaissance, consisted of architects trying to emulate the creations of the thirteenth century. The results could be pedantic and dull, but some examples stand out. St Barnabas, Pimlico, is worth seeing partly because its 'correct' interior was later richly embellished and furnished by Bodley, Comper and others. St Barnabas's was an Anglo-Catholic church in the slums, and the attempt to revive legitimate Catholic ritual within the Anglican Church provoked appalling 'No Popery' riots at the time of the Great Exhibition. The threatened closure of this church – in which Aubrey Beardsley once worshipped – provoked Sir John Betjeman's last public protest. The other fine example of 'correct' Gothic is what is now the University of London's church opposite Dillon's in Gordon Square but which was originally the Catholic Apostolic church – the principal London building of a remarkable Victorian sect whose origins and elaborate, recondite rituals cannot concern us here. Designed by Raphael Brandon, every detail is copied but the building succeeds by its sheer size and magnificence.

The Gothic Revival only really became interesting when it became original, and the first manifestation of this is a church: All Saints', Margaret Street, near Oxford Circus, the masterpiece of William Butterfield. In this fashionable, central church of the Oxford Movement, Butterfield attempted 'to give dignity to brick' and, inside, experiment with his theories about permanent colour and decoration. The result is a dark, rich, personal, polychromatic dream which many have found ugly. Butterfield, in fact, in reaction to the Protestant drabness of the Georgian age, wanted to make his buildings 'gay' with colour. At the time, many found this shocking – as shocking as Anglo-Catholic ritual. Butterfield's other central London church was St Alban's, a noble mission church built in the slums of Holborn by Brooke Market. Its extraordinarily powerful and strange brick tower survives but the interior was gutted in the Blitz. The new church, designed by Adrian Gilbert Scott and dominated by an extremely characteristic giant mural by Hans Feibusch, is very different but also very fine.

After Butterfield comes G.E. Street, architect of the Law Courts and arguably the greatest genius of the Gothic Revival. All his churches are worth seeing and those of around 1860 are superb examples of what the Victorians called the 'Vigorous Style': muscular, severe, boldly modelled buildings which reflect Ruskin's interest in the integrity of wall planes and his delight in the colour of Italy. At their best, such buildings are amongst the most creative in English architecture and were a profound expression of Victorian piety. Street's best is St James-the-Less, Pimlico, whose brick campanile now stands in the middle of the famous housing estate built by Darbourne and Darke, off the Vauxhall Bridge Road. The interior must be penetrated to see its superb carving, notched brickwork and general effect of muscular power. The same architect's St Mary Magdalene, Paddington, by the grand Junction Canal, is later and has more vertical and serene proportions, but is still full of vigour and has magnificent Pre-Raphaelite glass by Henry Holiday. In the 1890s, Comper turned its crypt into a medieval fantasy: a glimpse of old Nuremberg in gold and blue.

Many other churches in London of the 'High' Victorian years are worth seeing: the surviving slum churches by James Brooks, that master of sublime economy in red brick – St Chad's, Haggerston, or the Ascension, Lavender Hill, in Battersea; or the weird eccentricities of Edward Buckton Lamb as demonstrated in St Martin's, Gospel Oak, with its vast wooden roof covering a centralised space for Protestant, rather than Anglo-Catholic worship; or St Peter's, Vauxhall – a solid, dignified slum church, vaulted in London stock brick. This was designed by Pearson, the architect of Truro Cathedral and one of the finest churches of any period in London: St Augustine's, Kilburn Park. This is a vast building of cathedral-like serenity and dignity. Vaulted throughout in brick, at which Pearson was a master, it has double aisles and an upper gallery cutting through the internal buttresses and leaping across the transepts on bridges. This creates dramatic spatial effects and stunning vistas through columns and arches. A building like this is a product of high sensibility and also of passion and love. It is the sort of inner-suburban church created by the Oxford Movement where, as Betjeman wrote, the 'wives of the wealthy tore off their jewels and gave them to be embroidered into vestments and hammered into altar crosses and left by will sacred pictures inherited from their families to decorate the church walls.'

After the 1870s, the great crusade to make Gothic the universal style was judged a failure, but Gothic carried on for churches and with little loss of invention. Late-Victorian Gothic was usually in reaction to the self-conscious originality of mid-Victorian churches and often looked to the once-despised (by Ruskin and others) Perpendicular style. Windows of curvilinear tracery are filled by pale glass – by Kempe or Burlison and Grylls – rather than by dark, rich, colourful stained glass, and the interiors are tall, spacious and, above all, refined. Refinement characterises the work of G.F. Bodley, who is best represented in London by one of his last churches: Holy Trinity, Prince Consort Road, next to the Albert Hall. Here Late Gothic turns into the Renaissance, for Bodley himself is commemorated by a monument in the Renaissance style, inspired by that to his fondly imagined forebear, Sir Thomas Bodley. Then there is St Cyprian's (a typically recondite Anglo-Catholic dedication of the turn of the century), Clarence Gate near Baker Street, all white and gold and filled with elaborate screens, designed by Bodley's pupil, Ninian Comper. Or there is the Annunciation, Old Quebec Street, near Marble Arch, by Walter Tapper (who also designed gas fires for the Gas, Light and Coke Company). A fine suburban example, strong but serene, is All Saints', Tooting, designed by the true ecclesiologist's hero, Temple Moore. It serves one of the London County Council's admirable cottage estates built before the Great War.

Other architects, however, felt that Gothic good taste was not enough and that originality must be achieved through the ideas of Ruskin and William Morris. The dark, incense-filled interior of St Cuthbert's, Philbeach Gardens, Earl's Court is enlivened by beaten copper furniture by William Bainbridge Reynolds while Holy Trinity, Sloane Square, is a shrine to the Arts and Crafts movement. The architect, J.D. Sedding, a disciple of Ruskin, filled its light, spacious interior with sculpture by Pomeroy and Thorneycroft, metalwork by Starkie Gardner and Henry Wilson, glass by Burne-Jones and Christopher Whall, and so on. It is the quintessential church of the 'Naughty Nineties' and Oscar Wilde was arrested just up the road at the Cadogan Hotel.

Sedding also designed the Church of the Holy Redeemer in Exmouth Market, Clerkenwell, which is so Italian that it is difficult to believe it is not a Roman Catholic church. This was one way out of the dilemma posed by the historicism of the Gothic Revival – to use other styles. 'Back to Baroque' characterises the public buildings of the turn of the century and it also affected churches. Baroque reredoses might go into Gothic Revival churches – if they were of the Anglo-Catholic persuasion – although few complete Anglican churches were built again in the Renaissance style. One that was is St Barnabas's, Shacklewell Lane, Hackney, a simple severe mission church of brick and concrete with a noble vaulted interior, designed by Charles Reilly, who was to become Professor of Architecture at Liverpool. Another alternative was the Byzantine, a style made fashionable by that supreme masterpiece of the 1890s, J.F. Bentley's Westminster Cathedral. An Anglican example is Christ Church, Brixton Road, by Beresford Pite, a fascinatingly unpredictable architect.

The assiduous London church crawler will have consulted Nicholson and Spooner's *Recent English Ecclesiastical Architecture*, a superbly illustrated book of *c.*1911 which will take him out to such Edwardian churches as St John's, Upper Edmonton, the masterpiece of C.H.B. Quennell, father of Peter and author, with his wife, of *A History of Everyday Things in England*. The enthusiast of Victorian churches will set out for Stoke Newington or Camberwell having studied Eastlake's *History of the Gothic Revival* or that curious Edwardian work of piety and plagiarism, *London Churches Ancient and Modern* by T. Francis Bumpus. For all the churches in what used to be London, rather than Greater London, the Reverend Basil Clarke's *Parish Churches of London* is the best work of reference and it is depressing to see how many churches he describes have gone since it was published in 1966.

Such books are largely concerned with Anglican churches. I do not wish to neglect the Roman Catholics, but the literature is sadly inadequate. The Brompton Oratory, that unexpected vision of Baroque triumphalism, is a must, of course, as is anything designed by J.F. Bentley, the finest and most sophisticated Victorian Catholic architect. More obscure churches must be sought out, perhaps with the help of Rottmann's *London Catholic Churches* of 1926. Nonconformist churches are, unfortunately, both a closed book and invariably closed.

Twenty or thirty years ago, the brave, enterprising and inquisitive church crawler would pursue Hawksmoor in Stepney, or Brooks in Haggerston. Today, the true pioneer goes further out in search of fine and unappreciated churches, for the unexplored territory is the ecclesiastical architecture of the twentieth century. The outer tentacles of the underground or the electric trains of the Southern Region can take you either to wonderfully unrestored old Middlesex village churches – like Laleham, Littleton and Perivale – or to the churches built between the wars to serve the new suburbs. Here it is still possible to amaze a vicar by asking for the key, for it has never occurred to him that the church he would like to brighten up and ruin might be worth looking at. It certainly is; but this is largely uncharted territory, both in terms of acceptable standards of taste and information. Fortunately, these outer-suburban churches – sometimes clever developments of traditional Gothic; sometimes interesting experiments in brick and reinforced concrete inspired by

Continental Expressionism – were illustrated in two books published by the Incorporated Church Building Society: *New Churches Illustrated* (1936), and *Fifty Modern Churches* (1947). Go and see them: St Mary's, Kenton; St Alban's, North Harrow; The Good Shepherd, Carshalton; St Saviour's, Eltham; the John Keble Church at Mill Hill; St Francis's, Dollis Hill; St Thomas's, Hanwell; All Hallows', Twickenham; St Alphege's, Hendon – what evocative dedications! They are the works of such architects as Edward Maufe, Harold Gibbons, Cachmaille-Day; A.W. Kenyon, Martin Travers and the great Sir Giles Scott, designer of Liverpool Cathedral and the admirable telephone kiosk (which vile British Telecom are taking away).

Such churches undermine preconceptions about the period and maintain the standards of earlier generations of church architects. After seeing the Hoover Factory, go and look at the Church of the Holy Cross, Greenford. It was designed by Sir Albert Richardson, usually thought of as a neo-Georgian, but here he produced a streamlined Middlesex barn with an astonishing interior of great Oregon pine timbers bolted together. It was finished in 1940. And then there are the post-war churches . . . but perhaps we are not ready for those yet.

In the first edition of the *Spy*, Betjeman recommended both the best churches as buildings and the best churches for services, whether in terms of sermons, ritual or for sheer eccentricity. He observed how, 'those who recall the London of the 1920s will remember an even richer variety than there is now . . .' While it is still true that 'the great advantage of London churches is the variety of doctrine and ceremony and architecture which they have to offer,' the variety and interest has declined much more since the sixties. The sort of eccentric delights once found in old-fashioned nonconformist chapels and in the places of worship of other sects described by Betjeman may well now be found in the vigorous black Pentecostalist churches and with the other weird religions which have so often taken over redundant Anglican churches, but only Mr Roy Kerridge can guide us around these.

In the Church of England there is increasing uniformity and increasing drabness. The Church in retreat cannot bear to tolerate either eccentricity or adherence to tradition. Change to the various 'alternative' services and to a cosy, demotic, introverted sort of service is compulsory. The inquisitive non-churchgoer may well find what goes on in churches today baffling as well as repellent. The language of the Book of Common Prayer and the Authorised Version, which once permeated English consciousness, has been wilfully abandoned in favour of a dated, pseudo-vernacular, schoolmasterly jargon. There is much talk of the 'community' and other populist notions, but, in town, never has the Church been more remote from national life. All is now unfamiliar and only the regular churchgoer can really appreciate the full awfulness of the cultural disaster which has overtaken the Church of England and, therefore, England.

Londoners are fortunate because there is still a degree of choice. The language of 1662 is still spoken at certain services in several of the central London churches, such as St Giles-in-the-Fields, a bastion of conservatism. Such services are listed in *The Times* and the *Daily Telegraph* on Saturdays. Otherwise, most churches use the 'ASB' – the 'Alternative Service Book' – in which Rite A is infinitely worse than Rite B. Anglo-Catholic churches, however – aping Rome like sheep and therefore undermining any virtue in being *Anglo*-Catholic – use the *Missa Normativa*, a modern translation of the post-Vatican II Roman Missal which is quite as awful as Rite A.

What can still be enjoyed in the famous Anglo-Catholic churches, like All Saints', Margaret Street, is good music and elaborate ceremony. The conservative congregation of St Mary's, Bourne Street, off Sloane Square – where Lord Bradwell celebrated his curious marriage – still manages to preserve the idiosyncratic liturgy and stylish ceremony which people come from afar to enjoy. Also to be enjoyed is the music and the architecture of the 1870s; mission church Gothic cleverly enlarged in the 1920s by Goodhart-Rendel, guardsman, historian, composer and architect, whose brilliant neo-Victorian Roman Catholic church at Dockhead in Bermondsey is one postwar church I would strongly recommend. The highest musical standards are also maintained at St Alban's, Holborn, during services of dignity which, these days, manage to avoid being camp.

The famous 'Low' or Evangelical churches still maintain essential traditions even if the language is now awful and the hymns often ruined by the Reverend Michael Saward, the bearded Rector of Ealing, that poet of our time. Long, intelligent and well-delivered sermons can still be heard at Holy Trinity, Brompton, (right behind the Oratory) and at All Souls', Langham Place, the church by Nash at the top of Regent Street which has now been ruined by the financial consequences of pastoral success – wall-to-wall carpeting and a pulpit designed like a space module. Other, more modern Evangelical churches are more 'charismatic' and have abandoned structured services altogether in favour of self-expression and the atmosphere of a Sunday school. If you do not believe that grown men and women, who may well hold down responsible jobs, can possibly wave their arms about to the puerile lyrics of modern hymns, then try St Mary's, Islington, or many other churches.

If you have a taste for farce, or are still conditioned by the 'alternative' culture of the sixties, taking a schoolboy pleasure in shocking and in being shocked, then try the hotbed of Whiggish radicalism, St James's, Piccadilly (a building by Wren, restored after the war by Sir Albert Richardson). What goes on there, and in many other London churches, is described at length in *The Church in Crisis* (Hodder and Stoughton, 1986), a remaindered book universally execrated by both the clergy and the laity and written by Charles Moore, A.N. Wilson, and the present writer. And in almost all of London churches, these days, beware of the 'Kiss of Peace' – a product of the new liturgies, both High and Low, which is pursued with a ruthless enthusiasm which even the current Aids scare has yet to check. Perhaps it is better to stick to the architecture . . .

IDEAL HOMES

During the property boom in 1986, a greedy owner offered his house in west London for sale at a 'ludicrous' price, according to the estate agent handling it. What made it worse was that someone came along and offered the asking price. It was the nearest an estate agent, whose livelihood depends on just such people, came to describing someone as a 'sucker'.

The episode illustrates not just the greed and gullibility, but the obsession people have with property, which has helped to drive prices up to a point where London is beginning to be unaffordable.

But perhaps it was always thus. 'An acre in Middlesex is better than a principality in Utopia,' wrote Thomas Babington Macaulay in his work on Lord Bacon, and the search is always on, if not for an acre (since that would cost several million pounds in the centre of London) at least for an undiscovered patch where the process can start again.

For years, development in London has moved westwards, a phenomenon which seems to be common among European capitals. So when Mayfair and Belgravia filled up, Kensington and Chelsea were next for attention from developers, estate agents and ambitious young people alike. Then it was the turn of Holland Park and Fulham, where suddenly an artisan's cottage became a bijou residence. Even the Thames, a natural boundary, failed to stop the locust-like progress – Clapham and Battersea have now been colonised.

The most spectacular change in the face of London in recent years has in fact been along the riverside, from east to west, as planners and developers have realised the potential of building on the banks of the Thames, which has enabled the inexorable westward movement at last to be balanced by activity east of the City.

London's Docklands, eight square miles of it, has become the biggest building site in Europe (or biggest city-centre development as the agents would describe it) and its emergence from the derelict dockland wastes since the London Docklands Development Corporation was created in 1981 has been astonishing.

There are very few period houses in the area (Dr David Owen, the former SDP leader, lives in one) and the property is largely divided between recently built houses and converted Victorian warehouses. The former are mainly at the cheaper end of the market while the warehouses, converted into plain shells or sumptuous penthouses costing up to £2 million, are for the people looking for tomorrow's fashionable areas, for the yuppies, and for the highly paid City people, scattering like fallout from the Big Bang. It is the place of the moment and will continue to be so for several years – as long as the City remains a dominant financial centre. The big estate agents have now descended on the area, Chestertons, Savills and Knight, Frank and Rutley among them, and they do not expect it to fail.

At the other end of town, Chelsea Harbour is rising from the ground on twenty acres, and may prove to be the most impressive of the riverside developments. This £120 million 'village', which will have several hundred flats and houses as well as offices, shops and restaurants, has as its centrepiece a yacht harbour dominated by a twenty-storey block (tower blocks are making a discreet comeback). Its ultimate refinement, for the block that has everything, is a globe which rises and falls with the tide.

The owners who have everything are entitled to their little eccentricities, too. The Holme in Regent's Park, a fine Decimus Burton house overlooking the lake, cost its Middle-Eastern buyer more than £5 million in 1985. He had the certainty of having to spend more than £2 million to renovate it in accordance with the strict instructions from the Crown Estate Commissioners, and then must open it to the public each year. He has nevertheless managed to build not just a new garage, but a motorhouse for ten cars (large ones) or more.

Another Middle-eastern buyer, an Arab state ruler, bought a house in north London in 1985 for around £10 million through Knight, Frank and Rutley, and promptly proposed to install underpath heating round the eleven acres of grounds to ensure that he would always be able to drive round the estate in his special buggy, even in the depths of an English winter.

Overseas buyers of London property came in large numbers in the 1970s, particularly from the Middle East. That trend is now ending as London is no longer as cheap, comparatively, as other capitals, although there remains a steady flow of foreign buyers. The Far East is providing many of them, with Hong Kong a fertile source both for investment and for bolt holes nearer the time that it reverts to China.

In any case, most of the most expensive parts of London are owned by the great estates, Grosvenor, de Walden, Cadogan and Smith's Charity, and much of the rest will really be in the ownership of the building societies and banks through their mortgages.

The fact remains that people need homes, and that gives a chance for them to try and get ahead of the game. There are oases which still appear through the haze and are not mirages. In Hammersmith, Brook Green is one. It attracted those who found Holland Park too expensive and it attracted those from a little further out for the schools and easy access into the centre.

In five years from 1983 the price of a Victorian or Edwardian family house increased from £70,000 to £275,000, most of the increase coming in the last year, at the height of the boom.

Hackney has also seen some amazing increases. It is a mixed area but has lovely Georgian streets, and is near to the City. The next areas of London to fall to gentrification will generally be those adjoining the ones already subjected to the pine doors and carriage lamps. Brixton is a long-term bet, and Balham is striving hard to be more than a gateway to the south.

Expect to see more tower blocks, upmarket flats not Ronan Points, and as desirable period houses become more modern by the day, expect to see a revival of interest in between-the-wars houses. Any building with a claim to art-deco design is worth an investment now, like China Wharf in Southwark which sold out on the drawing-board, and there will be a lot of refurbishment of apartment blocks built in the 1960s and 1970s.

Property is a cyclical business. There are booms about every five or six years, and in between not so much a bust as a holding of breath. It is a question of finding an acre here or waiting for a principality in Utopia.

FROM PLACE TO PLACE

With People

But Not (On The Whole)

With Pleasure

UNDERGROUND AND OVERGROUND

What is this that roareth thus?
Can it be a Motor Bus?
Yes, the smell and hideous hum
Indicat Motorem Bum!

Would that A.D. Godley (1856–1925) were alive to add his voice to the chorus of Londoners driven mad by the inadequacies of the London bus service. Time was when the red double-decker was a symbol of Britishness itself. It ran to a timetable, had a driver and a conductor, both jolly, considerate folk who stopped for old ladies and small children and exchanged knowledgable banter with the punters.

Nowadays the so-called 'system' is in such a state that it would evoke discontent in Albania. There is no longer the feeblest pretence of sticking to a timetable. On the 33 and 37 routes in west London, for example, it is quite common to wait for an hour or more and then to find three buses proceeding in a stately crocodile. The crews have presumably been playing whist together in the garage.

There have been other 'improvements' of late, notably the abolition of ticket collectors on certain routes. That same appalling 33 for instance is now a 'one-man bus'. This causes serious disruption in Twickenham, for example, where hordes of housewife shoppers never ever have the correct change and can't find it even if they have to. In the old days the chirpy clippie would take care of such problems while his colleague in the cab got on with the driving. Nowadays it is the driver who has to spend hours of his day fiddling around with change. It saves money, but it leads to gratuitous delay – a clear indication of successive governments' prejudice in favour of the private car against all forms of public transport.

Even though the bus is less efficient, it is still cheaper and more fun than the tube. As far as timekeeping is concerned, there is no way any surface transport can compete with an underground railway as long as there are no bodies on the line. (This happens disturbingly often – a chillingly old-fashioned method of committing suicide, but showing no decline in popularity.) If your interest is in travelling as well as arriving, you're much better off on a bus. The 15 which runs through the City and Limehouse is considered one of the more scenic routes; so is the 9 which takes in the western Thames and goes from Mortlake to Liverpool Street.

Upstairs on the bus obviously affords a better view, but you may have problems seeing out as you are still allowed to smoke at least at the back of the top deck. There are no such problems on the tube which has been transformed by a total smoking ban and also by a continuing programme of redecoration in the stations. Sherlock Holmes is much in evidence at Baker Street and Eduardo Paolozzi's designs for Tottenham Court Road have been celebrated with an exhibition at the Royal Academy. Not everyone likes these rather drastic renovations. Certainly British Rail's equally lavish tarting up of the stations in its 'Network South East' has been more careful about the original character of the places.

At its extremities the tube actually becomes an overground. The Central Line goes right into rural Essex beyond Epping and Theydon Bois. The Metropolitan is as much of a commuter railway – a London tube which trundles way out into Buckinghamshire's Chiltern Hills. There is quite a pretty stretch of District Line from Gunnersbury across the Thames at Strand-on-the-Green and on to Kew Gardens. This used to be one of the few stations with a licensed bar. There was another at Sloane Square, but that's gone too. The green-grocers at Earl's Court survives in the middle of the westbound District Line platform which serves Wimbledon, Ealing and Richmond.

Travellers on the tube are less gregarious and friendly than on the bus. Indeed late-night travel under ground can be

'On the last tube home there is a serious chance of someone
being sick over you.'

hazardous as well as unpleasant. On the last tube home there is a serious chance of someone being sick over you.

Buskers are technically prohibited, but guitarists, tap-dancers and others do elude the policeman's net and contribute greatly to the gaiety of nations. The tap-dancers tend to stand at the bottom of escalators so that they can nip on the 'up' one as soon as they see the law coming towards them on the 'down'. Singers and musicians with ghetto-blaster accompaniment are usually static, lurking in the cavernous passages connecting – for instance – the Piccadilly, Jubilee and Victoria lines at Green Park. The most fun are the guitarists/singers who roam the actual trains, performing between the stops. An average performance will take in three stations. There is a heavy vogue for anything by Buddy Holly, especially if it's 'Peggy Sue'.

Despite maps, timetables, numbers and destinations written up on the front, bus travel tends to be confusing even to natives. They have an unnerving habit of suddenly terminating in the middle of Sheen or Ruislip. The tube on the other hand is brilliantly signposted with all the different routes given their own colour. The result is that the London Underground map is not only a miracle of clarity, but also one of the world's most popular pieces of graphic art. One authority suggests that it must have been looked at 'longer and with greater concentration than the "Night Watch", the "Mona Lisa" and the "Laughing Cavalier" together.'

No one, however, has captured the spirit of the London Underground, particularly in its suburban manifestations, better than Betjeman. Read 'The Metropolitan Railway', sub-titled 'Baker Street Station Buffet' from *A Few late Chrysanthemums*.

The Underground is part of a Londoner's language. The Overground is not – but should be.

The Overground is a far more extensive network of railway lines, operated by British Rail, but considered by most users merely as a means of commuting to and from the outer London suburbs.

Although BR produces its equivalent of the brilliantly designed Underground map, its services are too diverse, too complex for each line to be given a separate name in the manner of the Underground's Northern or Bakerloo (when BR did try, by calling its newly modernised services between St Pancras and Bedford the 'Midland Electrics' the press countered with the 'Bedpan Line').

Nor does it help that the origins of the Overground are in a score of different, often cantankerous Victorian railway companies, which is why BR's Southern Region operates seven termini. Logically these should radiate lines 180 degrees south of the Thames like the spokes of a fan, but railway politics of a century or more ago make the south London railway map look more like a web woven by a drunken spider.

Although BR, to its credit, now markets its London Overground services as Network SouthEast rather than by regions, the complete timetable still operates in a regional, geographical manner, starting in the east, where the principal terminus is Liverpool Street. We should not, however, forget Fenchurch •
Street which is one of only two BR termini not on the Underground system (the other is Holborn Viaduct). Fenchurch Street trains take the traveller via Cockney London through Essex beyond Southend (Central Station) to Shoeburyness. Its only links with the rest of the BR system are tenuous, which is why it has attracted attention from Tories bent on privatisation. At Barking one can change on to a quaint service that crosses north-east London to Gospel Oak (on the edge of Hampstead Heath); at Upminster there is a three-and-a-half mile branch to Romford on the Liverpool Street line; and at Tilbury Riverside one can take a five-minute ferry journey across the Thames to Gravesend (on the Southern's North Kent line). Passengers should also be warned that after 8.45 p.m. Fenchurch Street closes down and trains divert into Liverpool Street via a line not otherwise used by passenger services. The question now being asked, therefore, is whether Fenchurch Street Station is really necessary. The diversion to Liverpool Street adds only five minutes to the

journey and the real estate value of Fenchurch Street would add welcome revenue to impoverished BR coffers. From Liverpool Street, currently being refurbished, destinations are to the northeast and east: Enfield Town and Hertford East, Chingford, Clacton, and Southend Victoria. Stratford (reached by Southend Victoria trains) allows one to change on to the late Greater London Council's pride and joy, the electrified eastern portion of the North London Link (more of which anon). And in the rush hours there is an extremely limited service north from Stratford to Tottenham Hale via Lea Bridge. This must be one of the least-used passenger services in the metropolis.

Next door to Liverpool Street is a hole in the ground which used to be Broad Street Station. In the decade before closure it lost its services to Hertfordshire (now using Moorgate), and its connection with the North London Link, which now enters the City via a new spur into Liverpool Street (but only in the rush hours). And to think it once offered express trains to the Midlands!

Before moving west to Moorgate let us dwell on the aforementioned North London Link (*née* Line), one of only three Overground lines that has appeared on the London Transport map. Serving Richmond, just south of the Thames in west London, Acton, Brondesbury, Hampstead Heath, Camden Town, Canonbury, Highbury, Dalston, Hackney, West Ham and finally, North Woolwich on the north bank of the Thames to the east of the metropolis, it is the railway equivalent of a ring road. Some years ago, when it was still the Line (not the Link), turning south at Dalston Junction to reach Broad Street, its devotees tried to have it incorporated into London Transport, on the grounds that if seen as part of the Underground system its patronage was bound to increase. They failed, but not to be outdone organised a dawn raid and affixed transfers to London Transport maps at every station showing how the line linked up with five other routes radiating out of London. Before leaving this delightful line, it should be noted that at Gospel Oak (between Hampstead Heath and

Camden Road) it joins with the Barking Line mentioned above. Greyhound racing enthusiasts in Richmond wishing to partake of their sport at Haringey Stadium change here.

Moorgate is BR's most unlikely terminus, being mainly underground and actually part of London Transport's Underground station of the same name. But from platforms alongside LT's Circle Line it is possible to travel northwest to Kentish Town, West Hampstead, St Albans and Luton. It is actually a spur of the Midland main line out of St Pancras Station, but confuses passengers by having a station nearby called King's Cross Midland City.

Northwest London has yet to appreciate the attraction of this recently electrified service. Visitors to the Barbican Theatre and Concert Hall who live in Kentish Town still tend to use the Northern Line of London Transport despite the need to travel up and down escalators and await the right train, whereas Moorgate to Kentish Town via the Overground has two fewer stations and takes five minutes less journey time.

From subterranean depths elsewhere in Moorgate Station a service runs to Hertford North and Welwyn Garden City. Between Moorgate and Finsbury Park it uses tunnels that were originally constructed for Overground trains last century, but were used for sixty years by a self-contained branch of the LT's Northern Line that also called at Essex Road, Highbury and Islington and Drayton Park. Now the same stations sport the BR logo in place of the LT roundel. Because this line links at Finsbury Park with services from King's Cross, some intriguing cross-pollination is sometimes possible, such as through services between Moorgate and Letchworth.

The next station west after King's Cross and St Pancras is Euston. Its one inner-London service terminates at Watford Junction (connecting with the North London Link at Willesden Junction's high-level platforms, which cross at right angles over the low-level station.) Watford used to be on the LT's Bakerloo Line, but this service has now been cut back to Queen's Park (and Harrow in the rush hours). Watford, however, has its own network of branch lines: a diesel service east to St Albans Abbey, a station a few streets away from the main-line St Albans city station; and in rush hours only an electric shuttle to Croxley Green.

Marylebone is, after Fenchurch Street, the least-used London terminus and threatened by the internal combustion engine. Coach operators (aided by a road-biased Ministry of Transport) want to take over its route north in tunnels under St John's Wood (including Lord's cricket ground) and out into the open at West Hampstead as an expressway. This would require the diversion of Marylebone's High Wycombe, Princes Risborough and Banbury service into Paddington (where it used to go anyway) and the Aylesbury line into Baker Street (ditto). Three little-used, rush-hour-only stations, Northolt Park, Sudbury Hill Harrow and Sudbury and Harrow Road, and one rather busier one, Wembley Complex (by the stadium and conference centre), would have to close.

Paddington itself operates a service out through west London (Acton, Ealing, Slough) to Reading and Oxford. It also runs one train a day each way to Banbury via High Wycombe, which is BR's way of statutorily keeping a service in being without applying to Parliament for permission to close. Otherwise its London Overground duties are slight, but do include a branch that joins two LT Underground lines at Ealing Broadway and Greenford (twice hourly on weekdays, thrice hourly on Saturdays, but never on Sundays). It is also worth remembering that if in central London and feeling the urge to visit Windsor the rule that a through journey is always faster than one needing a change of trains is not true in this particular instance. Paddington Station to Windsor and Eton Central (changing at Slough) can be achieved in as little as twenty-three minutes, whereas the Southern's direct route from Waterloo to Windsor and Eton Riverside takes a minimum of forty-eight minutes.

Before moving to the Southern's sextet of termini there is another cross-river service, far less well known than the North

London Link. Kensington Olympia (once called Addison Road and the starting point for many of Winston Churchill's wartime train journeys north) is on the LT map offering an exhibition service from Earls Court. It used to be the summer headquarters of BR's Motorail, but now runs two services: the recently inaugurated BR through trains between Manchester or Liverpool and Dover or Brighton, and the irregular shuttle to, of all unlikely places, Clapham Junction. The three and a half miles take nine minutes – try doing the same journey by road! And soon to re-open, to provide another across-metropolitan service, is the tunnel between Farringdon (on the Moorgate–Luton line) and Blackfriars. This will allow trains from the east Midlands to reach the south coast. And, like the service through Kensington Olympia, this obviates passengers from changing trains.

The Southern's network is intricate enough off-peak – and too intricate to enumerate here – but in rush hours its complexities defy description. A host of lines that remain closed the rest of the day are opened up so that it becomes possible, if one wishes, to travel direct between London Bridge and Victoria termini via South Bermondsey, Peckham, Denmark Hill, Clapham, Wandsworth and Battersea without changing. One other particular delight is to work out how to travel the two and three-quarter miles between Streatham and Mitcham Junction outside the rush hour, which is the only time they are directly linked. Table 178 of the British Rail Passenger Timetable holds the answer.

But BR's Overground south of the Thames is not only about services from the seven termini. Local lines include Wimbledon to West Croydon via Mitcham Junction, and Purley to Tattenham Corner, which on Epsom racedays comes into its own, even being used by the royal train.

Finally there is one other Overground line that is actually underground all the way, yet operated by British Rail, but appears, nevertheless, on the London Transport map. Known by its users as 'the drain', it is in every sense, except its ownership, a tube train linking the City (at Bank Station) with Waterloo, gateway to the stockbroker belt. Quite why it never became part of LT and the Underground is fogged by a century of transport bureaucracy. The Overground, however, is still in business. Discover it! Use it!

AIRPORTS

It is entirely in keeping with London's prodigious appetites that, to service the bore-like ebb and flow of travellers passing through, no fewer than five international airports are needed. Five! That may seem a preposterous civic conceit but, in fact, not one of them is surplus to requirements. Indeed, such are the numbers wishing to visit the capital that the quintet – Heathrow, Gatwick, Stansted, Luton and London City – face a growth rate which, if matched by the national economy, would make us richer than Switzerland.

In 1985, forty-eight million passengers patronised London's airports. By 1995, the projected figure will have soared to eighty-five million – a total which, rendered down, would result in numbers equivalent to the combined populations of Brighton and Hove flying in or out *daily*. (If they were all on Concordes there would be 2,328 in the course of a fifteen-hour operational day, or one Concorde every twenty-three seconds).

A high proportion will use Heathrow where, even at the time of writing, a working knowledge of SAS-style assault and survival methods can be an asset to anyone passing through. A 2,700-acre complex lying west of the city, the world's busiest international airport was once windy, gorse-clad moorland frequented by wolves – the last to be shot in Britain fell in the area – and highwaymen; some of the anxiety doubtless felt then by innocent souls in transit may still be discerned today.

Heathrow is really a place best suited to the experienced business flyer. All airports make similar demands on the nervous systems of their customers, but here the pressures of crowds, queues, hectoring public announcements, immutable check-in deadlines and departure gates so distant you could write travel books about getting to them, seem alarmingly heightened and distorted. The less hardened would be better

advised to choose one of London's four alternatives, which
are calmer, cosier and more user-friendly.

Old Heathrow hands tend to avoid going there by car but, if
you must drive, allow plenty of time. The airport's Achilles'
heel is its access tunnel which, when bunged up (by vehicle fire
or breakdown, military security exercises or just heavy traffic)
can send a tailback reaching all the way to the M4. For anyone
running late this is a deeply depressing experience. Baggage
trolleys are not available on the motorway so you must either
run a mile with your suitcases or turn around and go home. It
is far safer to go by Underground. The Piccadilly Line serves all
four terminals, but allow at least an hour for your journey.

Heathrow's catering facilities are not highly regarded in fine
food circles – Egon Ronay called one of its restaurants 'disgusting' – but I have eaten passably well at the Home Counties
Buttery in Terminal One, the Runway Restaurant in Terminal
Two, the Horizon in Three and, in Four, the Four Court and the
Fourth Man Inn. These last two were notable for their pleasant
service and cheery decor though, when I last used them, there
were queues at both. While waiting for them to disperse, one
can wander through the nearby duty-free shops where the range
of goods available now rivals the high streets and includes items
like £595 bottles of Glenfiddich topped by solid-silver stags'
heads.

Terminal Four customers with small children should ask
about the free crèche. Supervised by four trained nurses, it
comes equipped with pedal cars, a climbing frame, Sindy dolls,
toy kitchens, My Little Pony sets and a Wendy house which,
since social workers condemned the name as sexist, is referred
to as the Home Corner. The creation of the crèche may seem an
altruistic move by the British Airports Authority, but cynics
believe its primary purpose is to allow parents to spend time –
and money – in the duty-free shops undistracted by bored,
restless youngsters.

The privileged minority allowed access to the Concorde,
Oasis and Executive lounges (where they may gird up their loins
before yomping away through the enormous departure lounge

to some far-flung gate) can enjoy original works by British artists of the calibre of Bridget Riley, Patrick Heron and Jeremy
Moon. More can be seen in the VIP lounges, though these became a subject of controversy when it was revealed that it cost
taxpayers almost £100 a head to provide tea, coffee and biscuits
for visiting dignitaries. (Journalists checking the VIP list on a
routine day discovered that it included no less than eight Saudi
Arabian 'royals', each with a retinue which, though supposed
to be limited to ten by Foreign Office request, significantly ex-
ceeded it.)

The airlines also complain about expenses incurred at
Heathrow, which charges a whopping £4,000 landing fee for a
fully-laden 747. (The same plane would pay £600 to go into
New York.) One US airline chief even accused the BAA of making 'an obscene rate of profit' but the charge is politely shrugged
off. Running a huge airport isn't cheap; and on offer are the
world's best air-traffic controllers and a range of technology to
match. Blind landings were pioneered at Heathrow. So was the
celebrated nut gun, devised to clean the threshold and centre-
line runway lights after they become dimmed by an accumu-
lation of nosewheel rubber from landing aircraft. To remove
the rubber without damaging the glass crushed walnut shells
are fired at the lights under high pressure. Such elegant attention
to detail is entirely characteristic of the airport from which the
world's first scheduled jet service was launched (the BOAC
Comet G-ALYP to Johannesburg on 2 May 1952) and,
twenty-four years later, in tandem with Paris's Charles de
Gaulle, the world's first supersonic service as well. So operators
pays their money and takes their choice. If they want to econ-
omise they can go to Gatwick, Stansted or Luton instead.

But not to the capital's newest airport, London City.
Located in the Docklands, its runway is a reclaimed 762-metre
wharf that Seb Coe could cover in little more than a minute and
a half and, consequently, only able to take smallish aircraft
with a STOL capability. The complex has been designed to get
hurrying City gents from taxi to plane in ten minutes flat –
and in circumstances far removed from the usual mass transit

arrangements. The customers expect five-star facilities and that's what they've got; the little terminal, efficient and user-friendly is fitted out like a good hotel. But it costs money to sample the facilities: flights to and from London City are Club Class only.

Businessmen on a budget would be better advised to try Gatwick – also the personal favourite of many frequent non-business travellers. Founded in 1931 as the home of the Surrey Aero Club, it sits so far out in the green Home Counties' heartland that a discernible rural tranquillity seems to have permeated the airport itself. The check-in clerks actually chat to you while even the customs and immigration staff are, by and large, unthreatening. The best way to get there is aboard the thirty-minute Gatwick Express from Victoria – escalators then carry you direct from the station to the terminal concourse – but motorists will find the long-term car parks easy and accessible. Buses do regular sweeps to bring them in for their flights, manned by drivers invariably patient with people like me who, back from holiday, can't remember where they left their vehicles; one, brandishing a jump lead, even came to the assistance of a friend who returned from Corfu to find that his battery was flat.

You tend to get these personal touches at Stansted and Luton as well. Both, when I last used them, had big vases of roses on the check-in desks and a relaxed, genuinely welcoming atmosphere. (They were also spotlessly clean.) The panic factor, endemic to airports, was barely evident.

At Heathrow, of course, panic has a very high profile. There, as befits a bustling city state with its own police force and one of the best fire services in the country – the night shift, forbidden sleep, may merely 'rest their eyes' – a chapel has been provided where daily masses are held, confessions heard and solace offered to the anxious or bewildered. In a newspaper interview the Catholic chaplain, Father Brian Laycock, explained the significance of his sanctuary. 'People *die* at Heathrow. They just keel over with cardiac arrests while rushing around carrying heavy suitcases full of worry.'

PEOPLE

ROMAN LONDON

London stands where it does because the Romans put it there. Down in the bottom right-hand corner of a triangular island may not be the most sensible place to have the capital city. Sheffield would have been more central. Colchester and Winchester were older capital cities. Oxford would have been more elegant. The rest of Britain has complained for two millennia that the position of London is illogical, and distorts the trade and communications of the rest of the island. But the Romans founded Londinium in the middle of wild, uninhabited forest, and there it has stayed to become an urban jungle and the greatest city in the world. Under the detritus of twenty centuries, the roots are Roman, the shape of the City and the pattern of the roads in it and leading to it were laid down by our Roman forefathers.

We know this from the archaelogical evidence, which shows negligible settlement before the Romans; and partly from the curious incident of the *canis* that did not bark in the night, which we have to describe as the *argumentum ex silentio*. In 54 BC J. Caesar invaded Britain for the second time, and led his legions across the Thames against Cassivellaunus and his ancient Brits. He crossed at Brentford. If there had been a crossing or a settlement further east at London, so careful a strategist and so punctilious a recorder of his campaigns as Caesar would have noticed it. He did not. When the Romans came to stay ninety years later, they founded Londinium at the first place up the Thames that the river could be crossed, and where there were dry hills rising above the lagoon that could be defended. Pretty soon they built a bridge there. And London became the great crossroads by land and river for trade and armies. All roads in Britain lead to London.

If you want to find the Roman roots of London, you could

take a spade and dig down about six metres into the debris and rubbish that we have piled above them. You might find some Roman remains. You would probably find a vivid orange stratum in the grey London clay. That is the mark left by Queen Boudicca in AD 60, when she led a rebellion of British tribes against the Romans, burnt Londinium to the ground, massacred the inhabitants, and threw their heads into the little river Walbrook, now an underground sewer.

You do not have to dig so deep to find the Romans. There are considerable and remarkable Roman remains visible still above the surface, but they are hidden away by the buildings of later Londons. It is possible and instructive to perambulate Londinium in the morning, finding the Romans in the most surprising places. You must remember that Roman Londinium, although the capital of the province, was small compared with vast modern cities. It lies under the modern City, the financial and commercial district around St Paul's known by the self-congratulatory stockbrokers and bankers who work there as the Golden Square Mile. Foundations of the Roman wall surround the City, and the name of City itself seems to me to echo a folk memory of the Romans.

A good place to start would be at the Tower, the southeastern corner of Londinium on the Thames facing sea traffic from Rome. As you come out of Tower Hill Underground station there are gardens with an impressive stretch of Roman wall, and medieval rebuilding above it. The Roman wall, built around AD 200, stood six metres high. At Tower Hill you can see the base of a Roman internal turret. In the Tower of London itself, beside Norman and later accretions, you suddenly come across more wall and a Roman bastion sticking out of the turf like menhirs, and part of the riverside wall built in the fourth century when the City was threatened by pirates and barbarians from across the water. The bastion was used as a platform for catapults that shot arrows; and a coin hoard, including a silver ingot, was found here, buried for safekeeping.

Opposite the entrance to the Tower, in the crypt of All Hallows, Barking Church, you can see a Roman tessellated floor: apply to the verger. Along the river front, depending on the state of excavation and the amenability of porters, you can still see patches of Roman riverside wall and wharf, the latter exciting as catmint to cats for carpentry experts, because of its joints and method of construction. The original Roman bridge, made first of all by a chain of ships, crossed the Thames opposite the west door of Wren's church of St Magnus the Martyr, with its inexplicable splendour of Ionian white and gold. They found a pile from one of the later Roman bridges here, and may one day find more, and perhaps coins and more sinister objects sacrificed to the river god Tamesis.

Not a hope of seeing the grandest building in Londinium and all Britain, the Provincial Governor's Palace, because it lies full fathom five under Cannon Street railway station. When it is eventually pulled down and redeveloped, we shall find many more Roman remains underneath.

I should leave the river and turn right up Queen Street to Queen Victoria Street to see the mosaic floor from Bucklersbury House, and the Temple of Mithras set in a little garden beside the roaring traffic. 'Mithras, God of the Morning, our trumpets waken the wall . . .' It was the uncovering of this temple to the chief rival to Christianity that woke up ordinary Londoners in the 1950s to the Roman past directly under their feet. I am afraid that you will not see the public baths in Upper Thames Street unless you have X-ray eyes or extraordinary influence.

At Blackfriars Station, where the black river Fleet still disembogues dirtily into the Thames, was the southwest corner of the City. An altar dedicated to Isis was found here, and the Roman wall turned north. At Ludgate Circus they found the tombstone of the centurion Vivius Marcianus, and at Newgate you can see the northwest corner of the Roman wall with a medieval bastion by writing for permission to the Postmaster Controller, King Edward Buildings.

At the Barbican you come to the richest Roman site in London. Under here was the legionary fort that garrisoned the south of Britain. You can still see numerous stretches of wall, bastion and turret, and in the Museum of London the fine Roman section with its large collection of objects and artefacts. You ought at some stage to digress from Londinium to the British Museum in Bloomsbury, where you will find mosaic floors and other Roman bits and pieces. At London Wall you can see the west gate of the Roman legionary fort on the first Tuesday of every month from 10.30 am to 12 noon and the third Friday from 2.30 pm to 4 pm.

Continuing your clockwise perambulation along London Wall (why do you suppose the street is called that?), you will find large stretches of Roman wall now serving as the north boundary of the churchyard of All Hallows on the Wall, near Irongate House, and incorporated into a restaurant on the west side of Vine Street. Unfortunately you will not get to see the mosaic floors in the Bank of England unless you are a friend of the Governor. The forum, basilica, and temple that were the centre of Londinium lie under Leadenhall Market. At 8–10 Cooper's Row you can see a good stretch of Roman wall with the medieval walls that came after. And then you are back at the Tower.

Londinium stayed Roman for nearly four centuries, until the fateful message from the Emperor Honorius in AD 410 that Britain was on its own, and could expect no help from Rome against the invading hordes. There is a house with private baths in Lower Thames Street that illustrates the decline and fall. It became deserted early in the fifth century, and in the ruins they found a Saxon circular brooch belonging to one of the new masters of the land, who dropped it while gazing in a wild surmise at the great city.

Other cities, even in Britain, such as Aquae Sulis (Bath) or Camulodunum (Colchester), have larger Roman remains, but I know nowhere where the Roman past is so closely and casually interwoven with the modern commerce and life of the city. London still bustles, as the Romans meant it to. If they had not come (and it was a toss-up whether they did or not), and made London, and incorporated it in a great empire,

Britain would have remained an offshore barbarian island, an impotent victim of the mainland for the rest of its history, much as Ireland was at the mercy of English invasion and exploitation for many centuries.

JEWISH LONDON

11 November 1928. Jubilee Street Synagogue, Stepney. Berl Rosenberg, a man in his late sixties, attends a service to mark the tenth anniversary of the Armistice. Later, on the reverse of the specially printed programme, he writes a short poem in Yiddish, 'To the Memory of My Son Isaac'. It ends, 'Only when I think of his strength and power/And of the work he has left behind/A light rises in my heart and mind/For that work his name will remembered be/As I write these words my tears flow bitterly.'

11 November 1985. Poet's Corner, Westminster Abbey. Ted Hughes, the Poet Laureate, unveils a plaque commemorating sixteen War Poets, including Berl's son. The ceremony is followed by a recital, set to organ music, of Isaac Rosenberg's most famous poem, 'Break of Day in the Trenches'.

As yet, however, there is no blue plaque to commemorate the houses in Stepney – or rather their sites – where Rosenberg once lived. A couple of years ago, I added my signature to a letter which petitioned an amendment to this omission, as a result of which there was talk of marking the corner of Smithy and Jubilee Streets. My reasons for signing were both literary and personal. You see, when the Rosenbergs were living at 159 Oxford Street (now Stepney Way) my great-grandfather, Reb Zelinsky, ran the greengrocery at 213. I have this fantasy in which the girl who was to become my grandmother meets this poor Jewish boy, a poet and a dreamer, who vows that one day his name will be in Westminster Abbey alongside that of T.S. Eliot . . .

Today Stepney Way has an odd, archaeological feel, as though the last denizens of the remaining terraced houses are leading subterranean lives while the real business of living goes on yards above in the high-rises. Whitechapel Library is still there, however, where Rosenberg and his cronies – Mark Gertler, David Bomberg, John Rodker and Joseph Leftwich – met to discuss life, art and literature. The Library, completed in 1902, was the inspiration of Samuel Augustus Barnett, a missionary whose chosen terrain was the dangerous parish of St Jude. Barnett, like the poetic alumnus of his philanthropic institution, also found his way to Westminster Abbey, being appointed canon in 1906. Nowadays the last echoes of those long-ago conversations are best heard a few doors away at Bloom's where waiters serve salt-beef sandwiches, hamisher cucumbers and blackcurrant tea to the multitude.

Two men became the self-appointed guardians of the Yiddish East End; the aforementioned Joseph Leftwich and the poet Avrom-Nokhem Stencl. The former edited anthologies such as *Yisroel*, the latter a magazine called *Loshen un Leben*, Language and Life. Researching for a book on Isaac Bashevis and Israel Joshua Singer I heard about their sister, Esther Kreitman, who lived in London and regularly attended (in the forties and fifties) Stencl's Friends of Yiddish meetings held at Toynbee Hall – another of Canon Barnett's legacies – on Saturday afternoons. They go on to this day, though Stencl died in 1983 (within a few months of Leftwich).

I obtained Esther Kreitman's three books – not to mention a first edition of Rosenberg's *Poems* – from Mr Hirschler, an extraordinary book dealer in Stamford Hill. His Edwardian house in Portland Avenue is a second Tower of Babel, a repository of Jewish knowledge, both divine and secular, written in a multitude of languages. Like his neighbours he is ultra-orthodox and therefore unobtainable on shabbat. Hardly less assiduous are Mr and Mrs Trotter who run the bookshop at the Manor House in Finchley, these days known as the Sternberg Centre for Judaism, which also houses a seminary, the Spiro Institute (for Adult Education), a museum of the East End, and a fine library. Incidentally, Stencl's papers are now divided between the School of African and Oriental Studies and the Taylor Institute at Oxford, while Leftwich's have gone to Jerusalem.

I am reminded of a mini-archive I let slip. Years ago I found on a stall in the market that formerly assembled in the shadow of Freud's statue outside the Swiss Cottage Library a Rakusens' matzo-box stuffed with letters. These were being sold by the recipient's nephew, Christopher he called himself (what a falling away of old values that name represents!). He also had piles of family photographs, beautiful *cartes de visite* and cabinet portraits, stamped with the names of all the cities of eastern Europe. I purchased a few from Cracow which I subsequently discovered – thanks to 'Fotografia Polska', an exhibition at the Whitechapel Art Gallery – were the work of Poland's most famous nineteenth-century photographers.

What remains of Spitalfields and Whitechapel is lovingly described in William J. Fishman's *The Streets of East London* (London, 1979), which comes complete with maps and suggested walks. There you will learn that at a Jewish Socialist Club in Fulbourne Street the Russian Social Democratic Labour Party held a series of meetings attended by Lenin, Trotsky, Stalin, Litvinov and Gorky. A more permanent feature of radical life was Rudolf Rocker. Not a Jew he nonetheless edited a Yiddish anarchist paper, the *Arbeiter Fraint*. His son, Fermin, has written a memoir of those times – still unpublished in Britain, save for an extract in the *Jewish Chronicle* – complemented by equally detailed drawings, which may be seen at his occasional exhibitions.

Let us end where we began, in a synagogue. The more orthodox the community the more atmosphere there will be. Men draped with prayer shawls hunched over siddurim, a smell of snuff and old paper in the air. But if you want to hear a sermon to gladden the heart of a humanist, best go to the liberal Jewish Synagogue in St John's Wood Road where Rabbi Goldberg or Rabbi Raynor will be advancing, with some courage, their own sense of Jewish ethics.

As for myself, I'd rather be at a football match. At Wingate Football Club, to be precise. But that is impossible. Once the only all-Jewish team in the Football League they have followed a familiar path and assimilated with a team of gentiles to form Leyton-Wingate. The past may be another country, but Jewish London certainly isn't, not any more.

25 November 1987. A happy ending and Emanuel Litvinoff, another graduate of hereabouts, pulls a cord to reveal a blue plaque newly mounted on the wall of the aforementioned Whitechapel Library by English Heritage. Upon it are the words, 'Isaac Rosenberg 1890–1918, Poet and Painter, lived in the East End and studied here.' He would have been ninety-seven today.

CATHOLIC LONDON

If you were to walk northwards up the Brompton Road and half-close your eyes as you approached the imposing façade of the great nineteenth-century church that comes into view as Brompton Road converges with the Cromwell Road, you could be forgiven for imagining momentarily that you were in the heart of Rome.

The newly cleaned and restored London Oratory (known generally as the Brompton Oratory) which was built during the 1880s and decorated in the style of the Italian Renaissance, in honour of St Philip Neri and at the behest of John Henry Newman, the founder of the English Oratorians, is one of the ecclesiastical glories of the city. The church it has most in common with is Rome's Jesuit church, Il Gesù, which was built 300 years earlier, yet, to my mind, the Oratory embodies the quintessence of Roman Catholic London. Congregations there seem to represent every nation under Heaven and anyone needing evidence that London is now Europe's most cosmopolitan city has only to observe those who gather in the forecourt after High Mass on Sunday, (or, equally, in the piazza outside Westminster Cathedral, or in Farm Street as Mass-goers leave London's own Jesuit church in Mayfair) to be persuaded that London is indeed a modern Babel. But it is in this fusion of the Roman, apostolic spirit of the modern Church with the old-established ultramontane tradition of English Catholicism, proudly preserved among certain families from before the Reformation, that Catholic London finds its most distinguishing feature.

'Faith of our fathers, living still/In spite of dungeon, fire and sword –' are the opening lines of a hymn sung by generations of Catholic schoolchildren. There are other reminders of the bloodier aspects of the Reformation in names such as

Tyburn, Newgate, and Smithfield where the Carthusians from the nearby Charterhouse met their death at the stake. Something of the spirit of the persecuted Catholic martyrs still lives on side by side with the reforming, ecumenical post-Vatican II mood of the Church in the fabric of central London's principal Roman Catholic churches built though they mostly were in the years following Catholic Emancipation in 1829 and the restoration of the English Hierarchy twenty-one years later.

There are approximately 750,000 Roman Catholics in London divided between the two archdioceses of Westminster and Southwark, and there are 112 churches within the London postal districts. However, a visit to six central London churches would perhaps best illustrate the diversity and the distinct Englishness of the Catholic faith in the city. First and foremost, there is Westminster Cathedral, the seat of Cardinal Hume and the English Hierarchy; begun in 1895 and constructed with 12.5 million red bricks, it boasts the widest nave in England and a campanile which, until Centre Point and other monolithic architectural disasters of the sixties afflicted the skyline, was among London's tallest buildings with one of the best views in the city. Still unfinished, the bare bricks await wealthier times or benevolent donors to complete the sumptuous mosaic furnishing of the upper walls.

Next, the London Oratory, already mentioned, where the proselytising spirit of Cardinal Newman and Father Faber lives on in the beautiful proportions of the domed basilican church whose Italianate interior is decorated with richly coloured mosaic and features solid marble columns and statues of the twelve Apostles that once stood in Siena Cathedral.

Farm Street is the name by which the fashionable Jesuit church is known to Londoners; it is Gothic Revival in style and, like the Oratory, is justly famous for the high standard of its music and the quality of the preaching. If the Roman Catholic world of Evelyn Waugh's *Brideshead Revisited* survives at all it is in the aura of this church and its immediate surroundings. I once met an elderly retired colonel after Mass here; he was dressed in tweeds and a Royal Artillery tie and his only home, he informed me, was a large white Rolls-Royce hearse in which he toured England.

St James's, Spanish Place, is another attractive late-Victorian church which lies close by the home of the Wallace Collection in Manchester Square (formerly the home of the Spanish ambassador), and near the site of the old chapel of the embassy which had been endowed by the Spanish Court. For many years it had been a centre for Catholic life in the city before the Emancipation, protected as it was by its diplomatic standing.

The original building that stood where the church of SS Anselm and Cecilia in Kingsway is now situated was also an embassy chapel – that of the Royal Sardinian ambassador. One of the most historic and ancient of London's chapels, it was here that Fanny Burney married General d'Arblay against the wishes of her family; that the composer, Thomas Arne worshipped; and that Bishop Challoner and Cardinal Wiseman preached. Alas, the original chapel, which had already been virtually destroyed during the Gordon riots, was demolished to make way for the Strand–Kingsway development at the beginning of the century.

The church that can lay claim to the strongest historical associations, however, must surely be St Etheldreda's in Ely Place, Britain's oldest Catholic church and the only pre-Reformation chapel to have been restored (in 1873) to the old faith. The beautiful thirteenth-century Gothic building is all that remains of the ancient palace of the bishops of Ely. Today it has two distinct congregations: one that during the week consists largely of local office workers, and another which on Sundays travel from all parts of the city to participate in the splendour of the Mass, to listen to the varied and imaginative singing, and to hear some of the most eclectically brilliant interpretations of the gospels preached anywhere.

Other noteworthy Catholic churches are St Mary, Moorfields; the pretty Church of the Assumption in Warwick Street, formerly known as the Bavarian Chapel; the cosily Dickensian church of Corpus Christi in Maiden Lane that is mentioned in Graham Greene's novel *The End of the Affair*; the beautifully restored church of Our Lady in St John's Wood; and the two Chelsea churches of St Mary's, Cadogan Street, and Our Most Holy Redeemer in Cheyne Row close to where St Thomas More once lived.

London provides ample evidence of the universality of the Roman Catholic church: the peripatetic churchgoer may hear Mass in Lithuanian and Cantonese, Czech and Hungarian; the French, Germans, Italians, Spanish, Belgians, the Ukrainians too, all have their own national churches and there are large Polish and Irish communities in Shepherd's Bush and Ealing, Kilburn and Hammersmith. There are also an astonishing number of Catholic orders, communities and convents throughout London: the Benedictines, Dominicans and Franciscans, the Jesuits, Carmelites, Rosminians and Augustinians, and the various teaching and missionary orders all have headquarters in London and many of them run schools of which the most established are perhaps St Benedict's, Ealing; the London Oratory School; Cardinal Vaughan, and the Westminster Cathedral School.

But is there evidence of London's Roman Catholic population in more secular aspects of London life? In general it is one that is thoroughly assimilated and blends unnoticeably into the social fabric of city life. There are a number of well-known members of both houses of Parliament divided almost equally between the two major parties, and there are several Roman Catholic members of the Privy Council. London has its own Catholic press: the two weekly newspapers, the *Catholic Herald* and the *Universe*, as well as the old-established review, the *Tablet*. Lawyers will tell you that there are certain chambers within the Inns of Court that have a distinctly Catholic flavour and there are families such as the Russells and the Devlins that have strong legal traditions. Doctors and nurses, teachers and journalists, even bankers, have their own Roman Catholic associations that meet regularly in London. There is the Catholic hospital of St John and Elizabeth, and in Pont Street there is the Challoner Club that serves as a meeting-place for groups that mostly seem to be old boys of the country's Catholic public schools.

The days are not long passed when to be a Roman Catholic would have aroused suspicion and hostility; today, fortunately, the cant and bigotry have largely vanished and no one raises an eyebrow anymore. The different Christian denominations preach and attend services in each other's churches, priests and nuns can be seen on the terraces of Wimbledon and Lord's, there are purple socks in the lounges of Boodles and the Travellers' Club; all the inner sanctums have been penetrated . . . ecumenism is now the order of the day.

POLISH LONDON

A blessing and a burden. A second- or even third-generation Pole, born in London, can be helped into the world by a Polish doctor, be baptised by a Polish priest, speak Polish at home, sit among Polish colleagues in an English school, go to Polish school on Saturdays and then to the Polish boy scouts or girl guides, join a Polish youth club and folk dance ensemble, go to Polish Mass, to the Polish theatre and cinema, read the Polish paper, travel round London in Polish minicabs, around the world through a Polish travel agency and finally be buried by a Polish undertaker (Mr Lysakowski of P.W. Ballard & Son, 308 Brompton Road, SW7). No wonder some of the older Poles hardly speak a word of English – even after forty years. But their children, while having the benefits and advantages of a dual culture, have also the schizophrenia of not belonging either here, in England, or there, in Poland, yet belonging both here and there.

He/she is what is generally known among the emigration as 'a Pole from England' – a concept which at once implies that there is a Poland outside of Poland and emphasises how the Polish emigration thinks of itself as being distinct from the population of Poland as it is today. The 'Pole from Poland' has been brought up under a Communist regime. He thinks differently and – until the recent influx of postSolidarity political emigrants – his motives for visiting the west were frequently considered materialistic. A cruel generalisation.

Poles – be it from England or from Poland – aren't the largest national minority in London yet they seem to be everywhere. They do not make their presence felt as markedly as do, for example, the Italians, West Indians, Chinese, Americans or Pakistanis. They do not own any great chains of national restaurants nor do they form a mafia – although

Ealing has often been called the Polish 'ghetto' – and, to all intents and purposes, to any other national, a Pole looks much like any European. Yet, to another Pole, he is readily distinguishable. Not because he dresses eccentrically but because his entire bearing reflects what many Poles consider to be their singular position in this country.

Although a few thousand Poles settled in England before, the main stream of immigration began with the Second World War and still continues during post-war Soviet dominance, especially during and after the Solidarity period.

The Poles have never been a nation to recognise the legitimacy of foreign rule and when the Nazis, together with the Soviets, occupied Poland, the Polish Government took refuge in England where it has remained ever since. Although the existence of a government in exile, sitting in its 'Castle' at Eaton Place, is an anachronism and might even ring of absurdity, Count Raczynski, the President of Poland – a remarkable and intelligent gentleman of over ninety, who speaks perfect English – is held in high esteem not only for his past diplomatic services or the fine yet curious figure he cuts, but also as a symbol of the legitimate constitution.

The majority of this postwar emigration centred itself in and around South Kensington before emigrating even further west to Ealing, Hammersmith and Chiswick, south to Balham and Wimbledon or north to Islington (although a fair amount of the Islington emigration dates even further back to the interwar years). It's interesting, come to think of it – the East London contingent is by far the least noticeable.

But numerous relics remain in their place of original settlement – Kensington and Earl's Court. It's amazing and wonderful how, for example, time has stood still at the Polish Hearth (*Ognisko Polskie*), 55 Prince's Gate, SW7. Although the club, which consists of bar, restaurant, bridge room, basement discos, and reception halls, is open to all and is not only frequented by Poles, the atmosphere is one of distinguished mustiness. The noble, old, plush chairs are chiefly occupied by equally old and noble ex-combatants who don't seem to have moved from them for umpteen years except, perhaps, to slowly shuffle over to the adjoining spacious dining-room where they can feed on delicious Polish dishes such as *flaczki* (tripe), *barszcz* (beetroot soup), *kolduny* (dumplings of mutton in consommé) . . . They reminisce, live in their own world, in the hope of an independent Poland for which they fought, and continue to address themselves by the ranks of an army which no longer exists – 'General', 'Colonel' and only the occasional 'Private'. Back at the bar, vast, ornate wall mirrors reflect shelves stocked with numerous Polish vodka, while Polish beer is kept refrigerated. No Polish wine – it doesn't exist.

Also in South Kensington (20 Thurlow Street, SW7) is the patisserie restaurant Daquise – a French derivative of the founder's name, Dakowski. Maybe he thought a French name less ostentatious yet more attractive? The pastries are good and fresh but the atmosphere is conservative yet somehow lacking in obvious historicity. In decoration, it is a coffee house like any other. But the restaurant does serve many dishes dear to the Polish stomach – like *schabowy* (roast pork), *zrazy* (slices of beef braised and rolled around bacon) . . .

But if it's real history you want, then the Sikorski Museum (20 Prince's Gate, SW7) is a small yet rich and concentrated source stocked with the inanimate relics of Polish military history. The numerous rooms are lined with glittering armours, the colourful uniform of Kosciuszko's army and the grey torn remnants of Second World War uniforms. There is a vast array of medals and arms, to name but a few exhibits, while, on the documentation side, the library and photo/film archives contain a wealth of information about the Second World War.

Still in South Kensington, just one more place comes to mind: Brompton Oratory. Here Polish Masses used to be regularly celebrated and now, in the neighbouring Little Oratory, a bright young Polish priest offers Mass and interesting sermons in Polish every Sunday evening at 6.

The fact that Poland, for the past 1,000 years has identified herself very closely with the Catholic Church is reflected even in Polish London. Where there's a large Polish community, there a Catholic church is sure to spring up. This is nowhere better illustrated than in Ealing where the Polish parish has just bought a large old church together with hall, while additional Mass is still said in the large Benedictine Abbey. The Marian Fathers' home and headquarters is also a place where parishioners gather socially over bridge, drinks, coffee, the occasional dance or jumble sale. North London, too, has its Polish parish in Islington – the oldest Polish parish in London, south London in Balham and Wimbledon, to mention but a few. And these, needless to say, cut across English parish boundaries.

In order to keep the Polish culture and language alive, Polish Saturday Schools have grown up alongside many of the parishes. Here, qualified Polish teachers instruct the children to read and write in their mother tongue, Polish history, literature and geography. Although going to school while other children play seems unfair, many youngsters later profit from this additional language and attend college classes leading up to O- and A-level standards. The Marian Fathers even run a Polish boarding school for boys at Henley-on-Thames, although English is now chiefly used. This school, incidentally, is housed in a museum of old Polish armaments.

It's curious, too, how Polish parents tend to send their children to the same English – usually Catholic – schools. You just have to finger through the attendance registers to see how many names end in -ski, -cz, or the like, in, for example, St Gregory's Primary School, Sacred Heart, Gumley House, Gunnersbury, Cardinal Vaughan or St Benedict's.

The newest yet largest Polish Social and Cultural Centre (POSK) is geographically independent of any church and stands proud and ugly at 238–246 King Street, W6. Although the amenities are potentially attractive, the actual Centre is exceptionally unattractive suggesting more a formal institutional atmosphere than one of human warmth let alone intimacy. This is acceptable as far as the library – run by most helpful and unpretentious bookworms – or bookshop are concerned but one would expect a little more from the restaurant and bar. All credit due – the food and drink are both traditional and good, although not particularly cheap, but, personally, I consider the general ambience of eating places to be important and here POSK does not score high. The Centre also has a cinema-cum-theatre with instantaneous translation through headphones but, again, the auditorium leaves much to be desired.

To drift away from centres – not all Poles like to identify with their national community. Numerous artists, for example, rarely put in an appearance at any of these emigrant localities. While remaining true to their Polish origins and temperaments, some have chosen to live in London and not on the isolated island of 'Polish London'. Such are the political cartoonist Andrzej Krauze and his painter wife, Malgosia, the graphic artist Andrzej Klimowski and his wife, Danusia, who creates disturbingly beautiful masks and three-dimensional paintings. Such are the eccentric elderly writer and illustrator team, Stefan and Franciszka Themerson, or the painters Felix Topolski and Marian Kratochwil; the film-makers: Jerzy Skolimowski of *Deep End* and *Moonlighting* (who, I believe, is on the point of settling in Los Angeles), Witold and Danusia Stok, Tomasz Pobog-Malinowski; the actor Wladek Shejbal (*Women in Love, The Boyfriend, Shogun*) and the actress Rula Lenska – to mention but a few. Or there are those who collect and exhibit the work of others. There are the Drian Galleries, 5/7 Porchester Place, W2, the Jablonski Gallery, 16 Woodstock Street, W1, or the Centaur Gallery, 82 Highgate High Street, N6, which houses Jan and Diana Wieliczko's collection of curiosities, antiques and Polish folk art – partly displayed in a former pig slaughterhouse – and certainly worth visiting especially if you manage to meet the eccentric owner himself. (Even better if you strike up a friendship and get yourself invited to one of his garden parties.) Which brings me back to food and drink.

If you don't like the Polish restaurants or clubs, there are numerous delicatessen shops selling Polish specialities such as, ironically, you won't come across in Poland itself nowadays (unless, of course, you resort to the black market): *bigos* (various meats cooked with sauerkraut and herbs – the more times you reheat this dish, the better, so they say), *golabki* (meat with rice rolled up in cabbage leaves), *pierozki* (meat dumplings). Delicatessen Stores, 161 Northfield Avenue, W13, for example, sells delicious sauerkraut – or rather *kiszona kapusta* – straight from the barrel and ready home-made Polish dishes. Then there's the Parade Delicatessen, 8 Central Buildings, W5 (expensive) or Prima, 192 North End Road, W14 (small but extremely well stocked not only with food but also with an exceptional choice of original vodkas). I could go on . . .

There are also Polish chemists, furniture shops, record and bookshops, the best and oldest of which is Orbis in Earl's Court, 66 Kenway Road, where numerous records, periodicals, newspapers and books in the Polish language published in Poland and other countries, can be bought directly or ordered.

The Polish comunity has organised itself so well within its own world that it has its own religious publications, *Veritas*, and even its own daily paper, the *Dziennik Polski*, printed in the native tongue and carrying a distinct flavour of 'emigration'. It is the only foreign daily printed in England.

Finally, if you want to go to Poland – Poland on the Baltic, not the Thames – apart from a ticket you do, of course, need a visa. Any one of the Polish travel agencies (Tazab Travel, 273 Old Brompton Road, SW5, Fregata Travel Ltd, 100 Dean Street, W1 are the friendliest) can get one for you – at a commission, naturally – or you can get one yourself and have a foretaste of Poland as it now is under Communist rule. The visa section of the Polish Embassy is small, stuffy, physically hot, yet cold in all other respects – and the queue is always very, very long . . . But just think of the delicious tripe, the herrings and *pierozki* in Polish London, all washed down with ice cold vodka – *Na Zdrowie*.

EXPATS' LONDON

Many foreigners regard London as the Emerald City in Oz when they first arrive on these shores. It is impossible to describe adequately to British people the enormous emotional excitement that most of us experience when we sit under the tree in Hampstead where Keats heard the nightingale and wrote his ode, or even walk through Abbey Road studios and try to imagine the Beatles recording there.

The faces that once stared out coldly from school textbooks in faraway countries now seem to smile down benignly from the walls of the National Portrait Gallery. And the initial sensation is – well – nothing short of magic. After all, the English language (together with its culture and history) must be one of the most studied in the world.

But, just like Dorothy, your initial euphoria at the Emerald City palls and you begin to cry 'I want to go home'. For many expatriates, especially those with preconceptions of London, find the cut and thrust of the city intimidating. This is especially disconcerting for native English speakers like Australians, New Zealanders, Canadians and Americans who tend to think that 'England is just like home but cuter'.

When trying to articulate and account for these difficulties, a lot of nonsense is talked about the differences in our mutual speech and spelling, that we are 'two cultures divided by a common language'. However, I must concede that in certain situations speech can cause problems. A dynamic young American woman with an MBA from New York University was walking through Chelsea when a Cockney-accented youth invited passers-by to attend a public meeting 'to free Soviet Jewry'. She sat through an hour's intense debate and as the people were leaving the hall she elicited some very rude responses when she enquired loudly, 'But hold on, when are they handing out the free Russian jewellery?' Spoken like a true American capitalist.

Up to one-third of North Americans and one-seventh of the Europeans who come to the UK on assignment have to leave before their contract expires because they are unable to adapt. At the root of the difficulty – homesickness and disorientation aside – is the foreigner's dilemma in knowing how to make friends in such a large metropolis – something that confounds most British people, too, when they come to London.

Typically, you don't get to know your London neighbours – a fact which traumatises most newcomers. This feeling of isolation is compounded by the odd hostile remark from people who don't like foreigners, and so one is left feeling unsure as to how one should proceed in making friends. There are people who come for years, adore their time here but never actually get to know any Londoners.

But the happiest expatriates are always those who have integrated and who can see that far from being hostile or indifferent, many Londoners are shy or apprehensive at being the first to extend their hands in friendship. They tend to see foreigners in a caricatured light: Americans and Australians are brimming with native self-confidence, Arabs are rich and Asians are cliquish. In the end, the conclusion many Londoners draw is 'why should they want to know me?'

It is only after living in London for a few years that the solution begins to become apparent; join organisations if you want to make friends. At ILEA classes barriers are broken down over a pottery wheel or a mixing bowl of crème brûlée. Voluntary and charitable groups not only make you a part of the community but they, too, provide an opportunity to get to know Londoners.

Joining one of the hundreds of expatriate groups can also be an effective way of settling into a happy way of life. It would appear that there are organisations for everything from political parties to the Petroleum Wives' Club. Not only will you be able to mix with people who understand your position

'. . . join organisations if you want to make friends.'

but will also be able to give you some excellent practical advice. Many a foreigner has made his fortune through these groups. But remember, it is important not to immerse yourself completely in a subculture.

Learning to find your feet in London can be greatly helped if you contact Focus (47–49 Gower Street, WC1 [631 4367]) which is a superb expatriate organisation with an information line. Their extensive card-index system of useful groups and individuals, as well as courses and conferences, can tell you all you need to know about moving to London.

Gradually, most people settle into their lives in London and learn to adapt. Adapting doesn't mean that you turn into a pseudo Bertie Wooster or Barbara Cartland, rather that you retain your own identity but throw off those customs from your own country that British people find objectionable. Saying 'please' and 'thank you', waiting your turn, not being a slave-driving boss; doing all of these things can have an enormous impact upon how you are perceived and treated as an expatriate in the UK.

However, not only do most people adapt, but they come to adore London and all that it has to offer. There are numerous expatriates who have come to London and found fame and fortune, among them: Egon Ronay, the gourmet from Hungary, and Bob Geldof (who needs no introduction), Sade the Nigerian singer, Paul Theroux, the American writer, and Lord Forte, the Italian owner of Trust House Forte. Ironically, one of the most famous, or perhaps infamous, commentators on the 'London Scene' is Nigel Dempster, who hails from Australia.

And so, for most expatriates when the UK assignment ends or academic course concludes, they are dragged kicking and screaming from the city they have come to love so much. As one New York executive fumes 'Would *you* want to return to a city where they don't deliver milk, the doctors don't make house calls and the police carry guns?'

As one Japanese housewife wails, 'London might be a city, but unlike Tokyo, at least here there are parks and space for my children to play.' 'I'll have to get used to visiting a museum once a year,' says a New Zealand student gloomily.

As the balloon glides up and out of the Emerald City, Dorothy tries to jump over the side of the balloon and screams 'I don't want to go home! For God's sake, Tinman, get me a UK work permit!'

ROYALS

During the Christmas holiday of 1982 the Queen decided that it would be interesting to visit a supermarket. Setting off from Sandringham wearing her headscarf, and with a detective discreetly in the background, she underwent what was for her an entirely new experience. As the Queen was going along the shelves, a lady came up to her and said: 'My dear, you know you do look very like the Queen.' Far from being nonplussed by this, Her Majesty replied: 'How very reassuring.'

Clearly the supermarket bug is catching because it was said that soon after Sainsbury's opened in the Cromwell Road, both Princess Margaret and Lord Snowdon were spotted simultaneously at different checkouts. The Queen Mother paid a visit there early in 1985, but hers was more formal. Not only were television cameras present, but the visit was duly reported in the Court Circular. Royalty Watchers can still prove lucky in that magnificent shopping emporium. Lady Sarah Armstrong-Jones has been known to amble in there in the early evening, but looks angry if recognised by fellow shoppers.

It is hard to know how much advice to give to the eager royalty watcher. It is one thing to be informative. It is another to cause headaches at 'A' Department of New Scotland Yard, the police division responsible for the protection of the Royal Family within Central London. The observant can soon glean which route the Queen takes out of London and the present writer has on several occasions observed a royal car caught in a traffic jam in the Cromwell Road. This will not happen if it is an official visit, when the police will ensure a clear route, but if the Queen Mother is simply on her way to Royal Lodge, she gets stuck like the rest of us. Some royals travel

'. . . the Queen decided that it would be interesting to visit a supermarket.'

conspicuously in huge Rolls-Royces while others favour more discreet vehicles for informal travel. The sight of a corgi seated in the back window of a Rover is the sign to take a second look and maybe spot the Queen.

No true royalty watcher will be satisfied with such informal chance glimpses as those. And shame on the type of person who used to dog the path of the late Princess Alice, Countess of Athlone, as the tiny nonagenarian made her way each Sunday from Kensington Palace to mattins at nearby St Mary Abbots. The poor Princess had only her parasol for protection.

At the other end of the scale, if you want value for time spent waiting, a major spectacle such as a Royal Wedding will bring the Royal Family out in force. The most rewarding annual occasion (judged on a head-count basis) is the Queen's Birthday Parade each June. Not only do Prince Philip, Prince Charles, the Duke of Kent and the Grand Duke of Luxembourg ride in the procession, but the Queen, the Queen Mother, the Princess of Wales and others are conveyed to Horse Guards Parade in carriages. The observant will also notice a fleet of royal cars that makes its way to and from Buckingham Palace. These contain every available member of the Royal Family – not only the Gloucesters and Kents – but also more collateral characters such as Captain Alexander Ramsay of Mar, the son of the late and former Princess Patricia of Connaught. A position near Buckingham Palace is recommended and field glasses are essential in order to glance along the line-up on the Palace balcony.

The Garter Ceremony which takes place at Windsor Castle on the Monday after the Birthday Parade is the most splendid and yet intimate of annual royal ceremonies. The Knights of the Garter wend their way down the hill after lunch, resplendent in blue velvet robes, the ostrich plumes on their hats bobbing in the wind. The Queen Mother, the Prince of Wales and the Duke of Kent follow the Knights, similarly attired, and the Queen and Prince Philip walk at the end of the procession, followed only by a phalanx of Yeomen of the Guard. After the service the Royal Family return in open carriages.

Her Majesty's representative at Royal Ascot is less discriminating than hitherto when considering who should be admitted to the Royal Enclosure. However, even if not admitted, it is possible to witness the magnificent carriage procession each afternoon, and invariably the Queen and her guests will make at least one visit on foot to the Paddock. Such is the nature of the day that the Queen has been known to indicate which path she will take by pointing with her umbrella and the crowds separate to let her through.

State visits to Britain take place at least twice a year, usually in April, June or July, or in the autumn. Again there are carriage processions as the visiting Head of State is conveyed to Buckingham Palace from Victoria Station. A little known way of spotting a lot of royals in full evening dress is to wait outside Claridge's on the night that the Head of State gives his return banquet. It is traditional that he invites most of the Royal Family and they wear white tie or evening dress with tiaras. Those that have been decorated during the visit wear their new prizes so if it is a remote country, you might see the Queen draped in a garish yellow moiré silk order, rather than the more traditional blue Garter riband.

Helpfully the Court pages of the *Independent*, the *Daily Telegraph* and the *Times* inform their readers where members of the Royal Family are to perform their duties each day. Small crowds invariably gather, but there must have been many an occasion when a minor member of the family has entered a charity headquarters totally unobserved. Obviously if royalty and stars combine as at a gala film première in Leicester Square, then the crowds tend to be thicker. It is even possible to undertake some royal spotting on a visit to the opera. Unless it is a very grand affair, visiting royals sit in the Royal Box at the extreme right of Covent Garden's grand tier. The Prince and Princess of Wales are regular attenders, but usually wait until the lights go down before taking their seats. A glance should also be given to the more central grand-tier seats where Princess Alexandra and the Kents are sometimes seated.

If you become a Friend of St Paul's Cathedral, you will be able to attend their annual service at the Cathedral in May. The Queen Mother makes this a regular engagement and afterwards there is a tea. For a small sum you can be present and the Queen Mother will speak to some of the Friends as she makes her way through them.

Sunday afternoons in the summer lure the Queen and Prince Philip to Smith's Lawn to watch polo. The Prince of Wales often plays and on this occasion he ignores the public as much as possible. His father sometimes shocked the spectators when he played, for in moments of stress he revealed a comprehensive vocabulary of quarter-deck oaths. The Prince of Wales is less nautical in this respect, but there are still difficult moments.

If you suffer from a desperate need to see a royal person more regularly, then it is worth recalling that the Queen, Prince Philip and Princess Anne use Buckingham Palace as their London base, the Queen Mother is down the road at Clarence House, and the Kents round the corner at York House, St James's Palace. The Waleses, Princess Margaret, all the Gloucesters and Prince and Princess Michael live at Kensington Palace. By and large they emerge from their dwellings by car, though they might elude you by leaving by helicopter. This red bird will suddenly emerge between the high buildings, taking its royal charge away.

BROADCASTERS

Broadcaster's London is, appropriately, dominated by Broadcasting House. The outlines of this building, at the top of Portland Place, had been so often compared to the shape of an ocean liner, that Noel Coward, in the song 'Bad Times Just Around the Corner', could confidently talk about the rats leaving it.

And the rats continue to leave the BBC. Higher-level rats either leave suddenly for rival networks or leave suddenly because they've been dumped. Lower-level rats, on the whole, just *talk* about leaving. This is the favourite staff occupation, and dreams of leaving can be heard any night in the BBC Club, now (since the sale of the old Langham Hotel) uncomfortably perched in Western House, the building which used to contain the Sound Effects Library. The only sound effects heard there now are 'Animated Bar-room Chatter – Large Group', 'Staff Whingeing – Small Group' or, at around half-past ten at night, 'Drunken Footsteps – Going Off'.

The new club, like the old club, has undergone that process of institutionalised decoration which is the rule throughout all BBC premises. The Corporation never forgets that it is in part publicly funded and so tries to avoid conspicuous expenditure. This impulse is compounded by a residual Reithian Calvinism and the result is that all BBC premises are decked out in pale greens and beiges. Pleasing architectural features (not that there are many since the loss of the Langham building) are obscured by this obligatory drabness.

The food available at lunchtime in the ground floor part of

the new club keeps up the colour scheme. Worthy salads are available, together with hot dishes full of plenty of potatoes, sausage-meat and pasta. Beige remains the predominant tone. Downstairs, lunches are more liquid, and earnest members of staff may become quite heated about 'the Realities of Broadcasting' over their glasses of house wine (formerly called 'Tantine' – Auntie, geddit? – and subsequently 'Sans Fil' – Wire-less).

Other members of staff lunch in the eighth-floor canteen in Broadcasting House, which commands magnificent views south towards Soho and north over Regent's Park. The food is sort of all right, unimaginative but subsidised. The grill counter is particularly to be recommended for the sort of steaks and fry-ups which nice middle-class staff members don't get at home (also there's often less of a queue there). Slightly more discreet and quiet is the lounge on the lower ground floor, which at lunchtimes operates a carvery service.

The food in the various BBC canteens varies. As a general rule, the smaller the premises, the better the food, though Bush House, perhaps because of input from all the ethnic cuisines represented by its staff, is reckoned to have the most imaginative menus.

Certainly, the quality of the food does not justify all the gibes of BBC disc jockeys who, deprived of advertisements as time-fillers in their programmes, will say anything to bridge the voids between records. However, one disc jockey recounts a story which, though it makes no comment on the food, may be revelatory about the attitudes of the canteen staff. Arriving at the just-opened canteen counter one morning after a night shift, he was confronted by a lady who demanded, 'What you want – tea?' 'No,' he said. 'Coffee, please.' 'Rose,' the lady called off indignantly to some invisible accomplice in the kitchen, 'it's going to be one of those days!'

But, of course, as with most big institutions, the main bitching, machinations and dreams of leaving don't take place on BBC premises, but in a variety of pubs and restaurants in the vicinity.

Different departments have colonised different watering holes. You can usually bump into a good few studio managers (if they don't bump into you first) in the Yorkshire Grey in Langham Street; any time between twelve and three you should find a publicity officer in the Crown and Sceptre on the corner of Foley Street; though the Light Entertainment Department – living up to their image of unpredictability – have recently given up the Coach and Horses in Great Portland Street and the Stag in Hallam Street in favour of the Western House Club.

Then there is the George. Set on the corner of Mortimer Street and Great Portland Street, this is probably the most famous BBC pub, though its height of fame dates back to the forties and fifties, when the licensed eccentrics of the now-defunct Features Department would gather round and vie with each other in tales of how many times Dylan Thomas had been sick over their sports jackets. Those heady days are past, but it's still rare during opening hours for the George not to contain someone connected with the BBC. Actors and actresses are often seen in there – particularly those who belong to that company whose name has been changed but which is still thought of by everyone as 'the Drama Rep.' (Their faces may not be very familiar, but everyone recognises the voices when they order drinks.)

And when the George closes at three in the afternoon, many of them will move on to the 'ML'. The Marie Lloyd is a private club in Little Portland Street, which used to be very tatty, but even since it's been tarted up, usually contains the same BBC flotsam in the late afternoon just before the pubs re-open.

Posh drinking – i.e. when a producer is entertaining an eminent contributor or celebrating being finally offered a job in television – is frequently done in the top-floor cocktail bar of the George Hotel, only separated from Broadcasting House by All Souls Church. Posh eating may also be done there, but BBC expenses are not lavish, so the more expensive local venues like the George, Le Routier (popular with controllers), or Langan's Bistro tend to be used sparingly, and staff home in on the Greek, Turkish and Italian restaurants of Fitzrovia. You can usually be guaranteed to overhear conversations about the revised pension scheme, the cluelessness of the new controller, and the essential bulletins of 'who's bonking who', in Efes, the Montebello and the Venice in Great Portland Street, or, moving east, in Ttokos or the Monte Bianco in Cleveland Street.

Further afield, BBC staff being offered jobs at Channel Four are quite likely to be propositioned at the Villa Carlotta in Charlotte Street, while those being seduced to ITN (or hoping to be seduced to ITN) will be found in Wolsey's Wine Bar in Wells Street. Thames and LWT tend to make their approaches in the restaurants of Soho (and some of the best eating, even after all the payola scandals, is still probably done by Radio One producers being lunched at the expense of record companies.)

More distant outposts of the BBC empire obviously have their own locals. The Paris Studio in Lower Regent Street is the scene of audience comedy shows recorded at lunchtimes and evenings (also, for a time, the semi-permanent home of Hetty, the notoriously raucous 'laugh' heard on all radio recordings). The natural watering place for people working there is the Captain's Cabin, a pub which seems to specialise in aggressive Australian barmaids. And from the Maida Vale studios in Delaware Road (home of orchestral and rock recording, some drama, and the strange hobbits of the Radiophonic Workshop) the nearest drinking place is a tennis club set in the centre of a block of flats, which seems to exist in its own time-warp and appears not to have changed since the fifties.

Broadcaster's London is a small world. That's the trouble with radio – since it's all in the imagination, for most of the staff there's very rarely an excuse to travel more than a quarter of a mile from Portland Place. Be interesting to see what happens when the whole operation moves to White City and the rats really do leave Portland Place.

LAWYERS

Forget Dickens and *Bleak House*. Forget the courtroom shen-
anigans of Charles Laughton in *Witness for the Prosecution*
and all the tales you've ever read of famous murderers who
have stood trembling in the dock of the Old Bailey, to be
prosecuted or defended by the legendary names of English
advocacy. Forget, even, dear Rumpole, whose televised antics
at the Bar are so wonderfully entertaining – and, alas, so
misleading.

The reality of Legal London today is very different. The
quill pen has given way to the word processor, the wigs are
now made in Hong Kong out of synthetic fibres, and the new
courtrooms are neon-lit, low-ceilinged and furnished in shiny
pine.

The costumes worn by the barristers and judges remain,
incongruously, serving no purpose other than blind tradition.
There are still rituals and customs to be observed by those in
the law, but they, too, have now become divorced from their
original purpose, retained only to perpetuate the mystique
that lawyers have imposed on the public for more than five
centuries.

The practice of the law is speedily becoming like that of any
other modern office; and the once overwhelming, mesmeric
personalities of the law have turned into grey functionaries.

So what is left for the visitor to Legal London? Much, still,
of interest, all of it free, and the possibility that for a few
magical moments in a few atmospheric spots, with eyes shut
and a vivid imagination, Dickensian fog might again drift in
from the river to chill the very blood of the law. The time for
atmosphere is winter, preferably with drizzle falling and the
light fading in the late afternoon. The place is that small
secluded area between Fleet Street and the Embankment

which contains two of the four Inns of Court, Middle Temple and Inner Temple.

It is best to walk around aimlessly, peering through the windows of the barristers' chambers (curtains have not yet been discovered here) to see them at work, preparing tomorrow's case or giving clients the benefit of their expensive and often incorrect advice. The very lucky and the persevering might spy that other barristerial activity, snogging. Usually it's a male barrister and his young lady pupil (trainee); but other combinations have been known. Lincoln's Inn, a quarter-mile north of the Temple, off Carey Street ('Queer Street' where stood and stands the bankruptcy court) suffers from having fewer chambers visible to passing spies, but it is the prettiest and most historic of the Inns and should be strolled around by day. Just off Lincoln's Inn, in Star Yard, is one of London's few remaining outside urinals, a small, men-only, ironwork Victorian structure complete with Royal coat of arms. The last of the four Inns, Gray's, is the least interesting, from every point of view.

None of the Inns is particularly welcoming to outsiders. The Middle and Inner Temples' historic Halls can usually be visited on weekdays, during restricted morning and afternoon hours (but not over lunch) or, in the other two Inns, by asking for permission on arrival. There is, though, a chance of being able to slip in for a while during the lunch period, with the added bonus of seeing barristers *en masse* at their refectory tables eating their school-like meals. It involves dressing correctly (dark blue or black suits for men, modest black dress or suit for women), being outside the Hall's entrance between 12.30 and 1 pm, and confidently joining the crowds of barristers scurrying in for their eats. It's a lot of trouble to go to for a few minutes at most – there is no chance of actually eating or remaining there unnoticed for any length of time – but it might be worth it for an unusual insight into barristerial gastronomic behaviour.

Proper dress is also obligatory for a stroll around the splendid gardens of the two Inns in the Temple. They are

closed to the public, but with a bit of luck and a lot of confidence adventurous visitors might be taken for Inn members, authorised to walk. The other two Inns are more hospitable, their gardens open to the public over the lunch period 'for the enjoyment of rest and quiet'. Watching barristers in full eloquence is easy, though usually boring. Open justice means that anyone is entitled to walk into any of Her Majesty's courts to watch and listen to the proceedings, except when they're *in camera*. The Royal Courts of Justice in the Strand (usually just called the Law Courts) deal mainly with civil cases and appeals. The Central Criminal Court in the Old Bailey hears serious criminal cases, as do other crown courts dotted around London. Less serious criminal charges are taken by magistrates in courts like those at Bow Street, in Covent Garden, and Marlborough Street, which specialises in trying West End shoplifters.

Building the Law Courts drove its architect mad, and no wonder. The inglorious Victorian Gothic façade in the Strand is matched by a cavernous, gloomy interior hall surrounded by endless miles of Freudian corridors, countless flights of stairs (some leading nowhere), penumbrous rooms and eccentric alcoves.

This is where some of the great judges of the land dispense English justice. The Master of the Rolls sits in Court Three hearing civil appeals with one or two other appeal judges. The Lord Chief Justice listens to criminal appeals a couple of courts away. There are no witnesses, very little drama, and proceedings are conducted in soft, chatty monotones.

In one of the other courts (the central notice board in the main hall will reveal which) Mr Justice Michael Mann enunciates the most brilliantly precise and well-rounded legal phraseology around. Unfortunately he doesn't say very much; but it's worth an hour in his court to hear the kind of language that will soon have disappeared.

For drama, the Old Bailey is pre-eminent, though long past its salad years, pre-television, when crowds lined the streets and queued for hours for their glimpse of justice and evil. The abolition of the death penalty has removed much of the tension from murder trials, juries today prefer matter-of-fact advocacy to over-the-top oratory, and memorable characters among barristers and judges are few. But the courts which have played host to Crippen, Christie, Ruth Ellis, the Yorkshire Ripper and Lord Haw-Haw can still occasionally evoke some of its past glories.

The corridors around the courts of the Old Bailey and the Law Courts, and the courts' cafeterias where the lawyers go when waiting for their cases to come on, are fruitful gossip territories. But the often heavy security at the Bailey makes it difficult to escape being shepherded into the public galleries, where milling among the lawyers is impossible.

Legal London is a small, apparently serene outpost of nostalgia battling unsuccessfully against the demands of the modern world. Nowhere else in modern London can one stroll for so long among evocative trappings of another age, unbullied by the twentieth century. The stillness is illusory.

LITERATI

English literature is the nation's greatest pride and no city has greater literary associations than London. Almost a sixth of the *Oxford Literary Guide to the British Isles* is devoted to it – twelve times as much space as the editors give to Manchester. Yet still they say that from Chaucer's time to the present day there is so much that they can't list more than a selection, skimming through the city from Adelphi Terrace (Garrick, Johnson, Thomas Hardy in the architect's office at number eight; George Bernard Shaw at his wife's house, number ten) to Winchmore Hill where Thomas Hood began his *Comic Annual* at Rose Cottage in Vicars Moor Lane. Everywhere you go there are blue and white GLC plaques commemorating dead writers.

Speculating as to which of today's writers will be thus remembered is about as profitable an exercise as betting on the Booker but there are plenty of candidates, ranging from that pillar of the Literary Establishment and the Garrick Club, Amis père, through the young middle-aged group of which Amis fils and Julian Barnes are the best-known examples, to such unlikely London literati as Ishiguro and Mo.

The popular myth is that writers are reclusive solitaries but in London they seem to be as clubbable as Boswell. In both north London and the southwest there are informal writers' lunches (Fagin's, NW3, and Valchera's, Richmond) where bored and lonely authors seeking the company of similar figures know that they can find it on a certain day each month. The north London gatherings have a reputation for being boozier and more celebrity studded though nothing there has yet matched Wendy Perriam's graphic account of an Ann Summers' sexual Tupperware party which reduced the entire Richmond restaurant, including the surrounding expense-account lunchers, to a stunned but mesmerised silence. Miss Perriam is the only known novelist from Surbiton.

Conversation – as so often – tends to be financial rather than aesthetic. Such a typical event was Hunter Davies passing round a piece of paper so that everyone could write down their income from the latest Public Lending Right handout. So is the ritual argument about how to divide up the bill. Kingsley Amis' propensity for large scotches led to some ill feeling at his first north London lunch and he has not been back.

At a slightly more formal level PEN (the acronym stands for Poets, Playwrights, Essayists, Editors, Novelists) meets most weeks at the aggreeably down-at-heel Bohemian premises of the London Sketch Club in Chelsea. Michael Holroyd, Shaw's biographer and a prominent figure in the world of Lit. Commit., was recently retired as president to be succeeded by Lady Antonia Fraser. Francis King, novelist and theatre critic, is president of the society's international parent.

You can attend for £3 and there is a small licensed bar where you can get sausages and quiche and eavesdrop. Among the guest speakers in the 1986/7 season were Auberon Waugh, Mario Vargas Llosa and Lady Longford. Every year, too, PEN puts on a popular 'Writers Day' at the Queen Elizabeth Hall on the South Bank. This is a good occasion for spotting a few literary celebrities. The 1987 guest speakers were Doris Lessing and the Israeli, Amos Oz. For some years PEN has enjoyed a rather fusty, auntyish image which it is now trying to shed. It also does Amnesty-like work on behalf of imprisoned writers around the world and has a special committee to do this under the playwright Ronald Harwood's chairmanship.

The Crime Writers' Association, of which Lady Antonia was chairman in 1985/6, is another writers' group trying to beef up a rather fusty image. It meets monthly at the Groucho Club in Soho and presents annual awards (Gold and Silver

'The Crime Writers' Association . . .'

'Daggers') at a gala dinner at the Honourable Artillery Company. In the spring Cartier sponsor and manufacture the diamond daggers for very good crime writers like Eric Ambler, P.D. James and John le Carré.

The Society of Authors and the Writers' Guild are more utilitarian, less sociable organisations, though there was a strong social element in the 1986 SocAuth AGM where an unprecedented mass turnout of authors from the ubiquitous Michael Holroyd to best-seller Robert '*Majesty*' Lacey met under the chairmanship of crime writer P.D. James to indulge in the authors' favourite pastime of complaining about publishers.

The publishers themselves are in a state of some turmoil and disarray. Since the last *Spy* there has been a proliferation of new homes. Century now appears in front of Hutchinson as the result of the entrepreneurial wiles of Anthony Cheetham; Pavilion Books, owned by Tim Rice and Michael Parkinson, has emerged from nowhere to publish some of the prettiest books and give some of the best parties in London. Liz Calder, one of the smartest editors at one of the smartest publishers, Jonathan Cape, has helped set up a new house called Bloomsbury. It is a sad fact that many of the old Bloomsbury publishers are no longer operating independently. The Chatto, Bodley Head, Cape group are owned by the American company Random House; Penguin Books have swallowed Michael Joseph and Hamish Hamilton, moving them out of their Bloomsbury offices and down to – of all places – Kensington High Street. Saddest of all, Anthony Blond, who published the 1966 *Spy*, is no longer in business on his own, but has his own imprint at Quartet – another relative newcomer. Hodder and Stoughton, one of the few old family firms, which has remained independent, still soldiers on in Bedford Square, as does John Murray in Albemarle Street – the only London publishing house which gives the impression of not having succumbed to any innovative vulgarity at all.

But if there *is* a Literary London – and there are good reasons for thinking there is more of one now than for many years – then publishers give the impression of being an increasingly peripheral part of it. Relations between individual editors and individual writers can be perfectly cordial – witness such regular Garrick lunchers as the Editorial Director of Hodder and Stoughton or the Literary Editor of *The Times* – but when two or three London writers are gathered together in Fagin's or at Valchera's, the Groucho or PEN, the atmosphere fairly crackles when the publishing industry is mentioned. Literary London is not quite the same as Publishers' London.

The Gaiety of London's T-Shirts

Suck me – I'm a sodomite!
Lick me – I'm a lesbian!

NANNIES

'You'll never *believe* what we came back to . . . ! (Gorgeous daube, yes I will have a tiny bit more) . . . there she was, in my best Jasper Conran and . . .' '. . . One kept finding strange black men sprawling about in the kitchen at 2 am and one simply didn't know whether they were burglars or just the latest in dusky boyfriends! (Mmm, spinach roulade! How clever!)' '. . . so Jeremy said, "darling, do look on the bright side, at least this one hasn't got a brother doing time in Barlinnie for GBH!" (Yes, it is rather nice, isn't it! We get it from the Wine Society . . .)'

The ancient oral tradition known as 'Complaining about the Servants' is not dead. Indeed it flourishes mightily in London's 'nanny-belt' which now stretches from Clapham in the south to as far north as Muswell Hill. (Nannies, incidentally, spend an equivalent amount of time 'Complaining About Employers' and if little Tamsin's mummy does not wish to know that the local chapter of London's Nanny Mafia is being kept fully up-to-date on Mummy's gin-intake or Daddy's disgusting personal habits, then she'd better knock loudly on the door before interrupting one of the regular tea-party briefings.

There was a time of course when nannies were only to be found in any depth in Mayfair, Kensington, Chelsea and, to a lesser extent, St John's Wood, Regent's Park, and Hampstead. Rising house prices, the working-wives' boom among the middle classes, and the enthusiastic gentrification of Georgian slums have resulted in a spread of nannydom beyond those hallowed 'core' areas. As Mrs Smith of Nannies (Kensington) puts it: 'For a long time, nannies simply wouldn't go and work in Islington. But now Islington, and even Clapham, have become completely acceptable.'

There are few of the old, traditional *Brideshead* nannies left: most have been stowed away in the west wing in the country estate, there to knit in peace until summoned to the Great Nursery in the Sky. The new-style nanny is young, often trained (with a certificate from Nursery Nursing Board of Education), does not wear a uniform, and does not regard looking after your child as a lifetime's vocation but simply as a job.

She can afford to be choosy. A girl with an NNEB and two years' experience can expect as a minimum her own room with TV, her keep, one and a half days off a week, four weeks' paid holiday a year plus all public holidays, and around £60 a week after tax.

The Rolls-Royces of nannydom are the girls who graduate from the Norland Nursery Training College in Hungerford, the Chiltern in Caversham, or the Princess Christian in Manchester; the social class of such nannies is sometimes higher than that of their upwardly-mobile employers ('My God,' says one of the latter, 'Never another Norland! Tremendously bossy, confident and rather stupid Sloane Ranger who kept telling me "Well, at college we were always told..." as though the Norland was the bleeding Vatican of childcare!')

Others swear by Norland's and are happy to pay a hefty price for them: a minimum of £100 a week after tax and national insurance. The price also includes the unspoken expectation of a 'Dempster Diary' lifestyle involving swimming pools, horses, sunbathing in Marbella and schussing in St Moritz.

Where do London's nanny-hunters find these expensive substitutes for Granny or the crèche? Those who want a nanny with an acute sense of social status head straight for the Harrods of nannydom: Nannies (Kensington) in Stratford Road, W8. There they will be charged a 'finder's fee' of £245 plus VAT and (oh, too shame-making) if they're 'outsiders' who haven't been given a 'reference' by established clients they may well have to endure a little discreet questioning by the agency. 'There's a certain amount you can learn about an employer's attitude on the phone. If we suspect they're not going to be nice and kind to a girl, we reject them. It has to be a fairly arbitrary decision I'm afraid.' Nannies (Kensington) tells the girls on its books: 'Make sure that the children you look after look as if they've got a professional nanny. For example, their socks must always look absolutely sparkling!'

If social status and sparkling socks matter less to the nanny-hunter, she can find other cheaper agencies with, on the whole, slightly less expensive girls. (An untrained girl with no experience expects £30 a week clear.) Among the market-leaders are the Nanny Service, the Belgravia Bureau, and Knightsbridge Nannies. Since nannies are liable to go off sick/get invited to weddings/get homesick for Mum at desperately inconvenient times, the wise nanny-employer subscribes to Childminders who'll quickly plug the gap for her with suitable 'temps'.

However, the great Serengeti of nanny-hunters is the Sits. Vac. Domestic columns of *The Lady* magazine. Every nanny seeking employment the length and breadth of Britain combs it every Thursday. As indeed does every employed nanny, just to see what she's missing. Nothing strikes greater terror into a nanny employer's heart than the sight of young Tracy ('and I bend over backwards to keep her happy!') gloomily dragging on a fag and marking up the ads in the new issue. The employer may not be wildly fond of Tracy but she's appalled at the thought of having to go nanny-hunting 'just when Charles has booked us two weeks in Davos/filming starts next week/I've got to go to Lagos for ten days.'

There is an art to writing a *Lady* ad. The experienced nanny-hunter knows that nannies do not do non-child-orientated housework: if she wants one who will, she writes 'Nanny/Mother's Help required'. An ad like 'Nanny required to look after two children aged eighteen months and four years. References required. Box No. XXX' will get her no-where.

Nannies don't like box numbers, they like telephones.

Nannies want to go to a 'friendly' home and are highly susceptible to glamour. 'Busy fashion designer with TV director husband . . .' is usually a winner: nannies have instant visions of free designer frocks and Terry Wogan coming to dinner. If the nanny-hunter can't be glamorous, she'll have to be winsome: it may stick in the gullet but it helps if she can pen an ad on the lines of 'Hallo, I'm Rupert and I'm only two but very well-behaved and I'm looking for a lovely nanny to look after me and be friends with Maudie my pussy-cat and Susan my labrador puppy. Ring my mummy at . . .'

Living in London is a selling point: young nannies from the provinces invariably imagine that living in London is 'glamorous', its pavements lined with dashing Mills and Boon heroes. (An illusion encouraged by the fact that nannydom's most famous luminary is the former Lady Diana Spencer.)

The disillusionment is likely to be painful and will involve the nanny-employer in many extra expenses – such as paying for subscriptions to Computer Dating agencies, tennis clubs and Weight Watchers (Mr Kipling's cakes and endless tea-parties make spots and obesity nannydom's industrial disease).

An experienced nanny-hunter always insists on references and follows them up with telephone calls. She will be suspicious about a reference signed only by the male half of the employing couple: bitter experience tells her that it may have been written under duress. ('If you don't give me a good reference, I'll tell your wife about . . .') In high season throughout the nanny-belt, employers are scrutinising references for possible coded messages. 'Tracy has very high standards' may mean 'always wingeing and talking about her "rights".' Other 'codes' may lurk within the following: 'Tracy got on very well with the children' ('Sat them in front of the television all day and filled them up with Mars Bars'); 'Tracy is very clean' ('spends hours in the bath'); 'Tracy is a sociable girl' ('Staggers in at 2 am reeking of "substances"').

Nannies, poor things, can't demand a reference from a prospective employer. The nearest they get to it is an ad containing the gold-dust sentence, 'Present nanny highly recommends.' (Wisely, they'll check on that.)

Our spy at the tea-parties of London's Nanny Mafia indicates some strong likes and dislikes prevalent about employers in nannydom. Nannies do not like mothers being under foot all day: 'She's always interfering and the kids are always playing her off against you.' They don't like arbitrary cancellation of evenings off: 'Pete was taking me to Camden Palace that night and she rang to say she wouldn't be back till midnight!' They disapprove of non-working mothers with a hectic social life: 'She shouldn't have had children if all she wants to do is enjoy herself!' They don't like being treated as a status symbol, on a par with the Merc in the drive. (Golders Green's rag-trade czars are considered to be particularly bad in this respect: 'I have to wear a uniform and she always calls me "Nanny" in front of her friends!')

On the other hand, too much egalitarian chumminess can also get a nanny down. North London employers who read the *Guardian* and who still vote Labour tend to feel guilty about having a 'domestic servant'. Nannies do not find such guilt flattering: 'She always introduces me as "Jane, who's helping out with the children today". I'm not ashamed of being a nanny but she makes me feel I should be!'

The high season for nanny-hunting is just before the main holiday periods: Christmas, Easter and early summer (when the migration of the nanny tribes tends to be at stampede level). Surprisingly, children seem to survive the changeovers remarkably well: a previously happy employer can be devastated. 'When Sarah left for New Zealand, I cried buckets for days!' Full of foreboding, she heads back to the Serengeti of the Sits. Vac. of *The Lady* . . .

Stiletto Fashions (Chelsea)

Punk girls the skin'ead likes
wear their hair in spikes.
In thirty years, one feels,
they've gone to their heads,
from their heels.

TEENS

The Teenager is a fifties' creation but in London it lives on with greater vigour and variety than ever before. Some groups have survived through decades – punks, mods and teddy boys – but new strains of teen are always being developed. Some prove transitory while others, like the psycho and the casual, appear to be as durable as the teds and punks. 'Teenagers' and 'youths' seem to get younger year after year – you can be as young as eleven years old to qualify as a London youth – but the activities stay much the same: dancing, drinking, and 'having a laugh', which is as often a euphemism for a punch up as a knees up.

Probably the largest of classifiable groups is the casuals. This type of person is most notable for his/her unmoulded and unshaven hair. The only thing the average casual's locks will endure is a very bad dye. This is always blond and always leaves at least a centimetre of natural colour at the roots. One golden earring for the male (left ear if you don't want to be left-handed), and two larger ones for the female is common. The casual is one of the few groups of youths to have distinctive names. A casual girl, for example, is always (according to popular non-casual myth) called Sharon. The male has a more varied selection of tags, the most popular being Kevin, Garry or Terry. (NB: Kevin is always nineteen plus, brown-haired, and has a moustache.) When a casual is going out to the disco he will always wear his best pair of purple tassel shoes, while Sharon will always be accompanied by her trusty handbag, around which she will dance to the sounds of her favourite soul or pop groups. Ice rinks are another popular haunt at weekends, not for the skating you understand, but for 'a laugh', a chance to meet up with your mates and not be asked for irritating things like ID.

'Some pubs . . . will serve almost anyone not still in nappies.'

This last marks a prominent feature among the young – under-age drinking and clubbing. All London discos have age limits, usually eighteen years old. But this proves no obstacle – if you're wearing your 'high-heelers' and are suitably made-up you can make it past the bouncers. The more exclusive clubs, like Stringfellows and the Hippodrome are unlikely to admit under-eighteens, always assuming the hopefuls satisfy the strict dress code first. Smaller clubs and discos pose no particular problems – confidence and an air of purpose can guarantee you entry. Discos like the Kilburn National and the Town and Country in Kentish Town are really glorified pubs, and often double as concert venues. On a slightly higher tier come Samantha's, the Camden Palace, and Buzby's in the Tottenham Court Road – they won't allow jeans and are more likely to enquire after age.

Pubs themselves are very popular meeting-places – no entrance fee, and cheaper booze than the clubs. Some pubs are 'easier' than others, and will serve almost anyone not still in nappies. It becomes a social embarrassment to be 'refused' in a pub, let alone in front of your friends. Drink is often the focal point of a night out – who can get pissed quickest and cheapest. Success is marked by a pile of sick outside the front door and a splitting headache the following morning. On a Monday the air will be thick with claims that 'I was paralytic', and 'I didn't know *what* I was doing!' – real kudos.

Undoubtedly the most famous and colourful creature in the wide and varied zoo of London youth is the typical punk. Any tourist, be he American, Japanese or other will want to snap a sneering young man or woman with some sort of delightful concoction sprouting from their head, to take back and show the family what 'British Teenagers' look like. As well as the hair, (which can be turned into almost anything with the help of some dye, hairspray – two cans a go – and an electric razor) they could hope for black leather, studs, hundreds of zips and possibly even a ring or safety pin hanging out of the nose. Many of the more entrepreneurial of the punks have caught on to the money available in this and will

'. . . the typical punk.'

charge the visitor for the privilege. Goths are one of the newest types of punk, dressed in black, with silver buckles and studs, swaying in ethereal manner under clouds of hairspray to the music of bands such as the Cult, the Mission, and punk stalwarts Siouxie and the Banshees.

The teenage teddy boy of the fifties has mutated into two groups of teens in the eighties, very similar in style to the uninitiated, but worlds apart to those in the know. Rockabillys have stayed much the same; quiffs and jeans for the lads, ponytails and circular skirts for the girls. But a new style has emerged – the psychobilly. Psychobillys can often be found at Klub Foot in the Hammersmith Clarendon, drinking huge quantities of beer, and 'slamming' to the sounds of bands like King Kurt, and the Meteors. Slamming can loosely be described as a dance, not totally unrelated to the pogoing of seventies' punks, but every bit as dangerous. Arms and legs are swung in every direction, preferably at the nearest human being. Dress usually consists of faded and torn jeans or dungarees, Doc Martens of one kind or another (suede, patent, pointed, round-toed, steel toe-caps, red, black – the list goes on and on), and a jacket, often an American baseball type, sometimes a black bomber. This outfit is topped by a quiff – practically any colour, length or thickness is acceptable. Like any other 'group' in London, psychos have individual gangs – the 'London Psychos', with the name on their jackets, and the Wrecking Crew, who prefer to go incognito in order to cause as much trouble as possible without getting caught. Psycho violence can be directed not only at each other, but at different types of teenager. Any casual foolish enough to stray into the Clarendon on a Saturday night is likely to be subjected to extreme verbal and physical abuse. But there's rivalry between all genres of London's young – casuals and skins, punks and mods, psychos and headbangers. Many a route home can be decided by which band is playing in the local pub, or whether Iron Maiden are in town. Nevertheless, even a black eye can become a status symbol ('You should have seen the state of the other bloke!')

If the punk is the epitome of London youth in the States, then the skinhead is infamous throughout Europe. Possibly every country on the continent has had their football stadium and surrounding vicinities vandalised by some young Londoner with a shaven head, braces, and a Union Jack T-shirt, claiming to be a Spurs, Chelsea or even Liverpool supporter. It must be said that some of the worst football hooligans seem to emanate from the south, and from such notorious clubs as Chelsea and Millwall, though London skinheads don't always 'support' London clubs. In recent years, these thugs have found a new and very eerie angle on the beating up of rival fans: they leave calling cards on their victims. It is also often thought that skinhead hooligans are fully paid-up members of the National Front, too. The Doc Marten boot is a favourite form of footwear for this type of skinhead, mainly because it is known to be a useful kicking utensil. While skinheads compose by no means the majority of football hooligans, they certainly look the most menacing.

Hip-hop, imported from Washington DC, has bred another gang of young people, often blacks: the Posse. They're not new – the casuals often grouped themselves under such names as the Blondin Posse – but the music is. Fans of reggae and Lover's Rock, with their gold jewellery and large, styled black leather jackets also form posses, and are yet another grouping of youths commonly found in London.

There are of course those who fit into none of these categories. Many are merely young adults or elderly children, completely bypassing the stage of Teenager. Young Sloanes, the Hooray Henrys and Henriettas of the future, are the most obvious example. But, generally speaking, modern London teens can earn good money in temporary evening and weekend jobs while still living at home and being supported by fond parents. Since the sixties, at least, those same fond parents have come to exercise fewer and fewer of the traditional restraints on their young. Hence a vibrant, sometimes uncomfortable Youth Culture, which is here to stay.

SOLDIERS

London is full of soldiers. Not only does it house the War Office, in theory at least part of the so-called Ministry of Defence, staffed to a large extent by superannuated majors, and many, many prematurely aged civil servants, but also the Headquarters of London District, altogether more colourful and amusing.

The Ministry of Defence, commanded by the Chief of the General Staff, deals with complex problems, such as whose turn it is next for garrison duties in the Falkland Islands (the Arms Plot), can the proposed new Military Attaché for Moscow really speak Russian? (Defence Intelligence), down to the decision to replace soldiers' leather bootlaces with nylon ones – nylon doesn't hold boot polish (Quartermaster General). Ministry men tend to be married. Bachelors, unless they are notorious womanisers, in which case they are a security risk anyway, tend to be rather suspect. In any event, since the Ministry makes no attempt to house them, married or single, nearer to their place of work than Woolwich (believed to be on the Dover road) they are to be seen leaving London in droves between five and six o'clock of an evening, mainly from Waterloo, to their houses in Woking, Surbiton or elsewhere.

London District, not a battle formation but an administrative area (including strangely Windsor and Pirbright) is always commanded by a Guards major-general who sits in splendour in the First Duke of Wellington's office and at the Iron Duke's desk overlooking Horse Guards Parade and has a variety of troops at his disposal.

Firstly he has normally four out of the eight Footguards (infantry) battalions (Grenadier, Coldstream, Scots, Irish and Welsh Guards) and two squadrons of Household Cavalry

'...home of the 500 men and 200 black horses of the
Household Cavalry.'

(one of each of the Life Guards and the Blues and Royals). Then there is the King's Troop, Royal Horse Artillery, who, although living in suburbia north of the Park at St John's Wood and causing constant breaches of the peace by firing salutes at unexpected moments in the summer, spend most of the winter hunting at Melton Mowbray. They also spawn 'in' people – Ronnie Scott, the Cirencester Park Polo Manager, Bill Lithgow, a high-up in the British Horse Society, James Templar, our 'white hope' at the Tokyo Olympics, and Malcolm Wallace, recently retired Chef d'Equipe of our Olympic three-day event team. (His place is taken by a former Guards officer.)

The major-general finally has at his command odds and sods such as mechanics, signallers, engineers and transport men, who are by and large disregarded until something occurs which is beyond the capacity of the Guards to solve. They are then called in to rectify the problem, their officer perhaps being given luncheon in the officers' mess in Wellington Barracks (Birdcage Walk) or Chelsea Barracks – both Foot-guard strongholds, or in Hyde Park Barracks which is the home of the 500 men and 200 black horses of the Household Cavalry.

It is easy to write off Guards officers as overbred simpletons with a public school education, a braying laugh and a short-changed chin. True to an extent perhaps, but it was men of that ilk notably those of the Scots and Welsh Guards and the Blues and Royals, who in recent years, assisted in the recapture of the Falkland Islands. Detractors will maintain that their men followed their officers out of curiosity only, but follow them they did, to good effect. All the regiments' battle honours are a testimonial to the system, for better or for worse, which has worked over centuries.

So how do these young men, physically fit, many with private incomes and all in the knowledge that their stay in London will only be for between one and two years, fill their time between mounting guard at Buckingham and St James's Palace, the Tower of London and the Bank of England

(Footguards) and at Horse Guards (Household Cavalry)? The answer is that their behaviour differs only slightly from young civilians in similar circumstances. Most of the captains and below live in their various barracks and are to be seen emerging of an evening (leaving behind one of their number who has been detailed by the adjutant previously to hold the fort, metaphorically, with a small 'night guard' of soldiery).

Either there is a 'deb' dance to which they may or may not have been invited (Mrs Betty Kenward, doyenne for some decades of the social scene, has always been thought to hold a register of the eligible young men in town, annotating them where appropriate NST – not safe in taxis – or NSA – not safe at all). Or there might be some pre-arranged engagement with some girl for dinner, perhaps in the Kensington area. In either case the aim, which needs no further elucidation, is the same.

It is at this point that the Footguards (Woodentops to Household Cavalry friends in their unkinder moments) tend to be somewhat rigid in outlook. To them situations or people are either 'Good news', 'Bad news' or, at worst 'No news'. Thus an attractive girl who is reasonably free with her favours is 'Good news', the same girl, who is 'saving herself for marriage or whatever' is 'Bad news' whereas an ugly girl who is dying to give it away is 'No news'. An officer who shall be nameless incurred in his younger days the nickname of 'Bad news'. The story is perhaps apocryphal, but is still told in Footguard circles. The young man, having been encircled by the enemy on manoeuvres, was hailed with the cry, 'Good news, Bad news, you are surrounded!'

The Household Cavalry officers tend to be more flexible. At breakfast in the mess, arrivals are greeted with such cries as, 'How many points then, Ron? or 'Get it?' If the interrogatee is genuinely fond of his previous night's partner he will not answer – if however the girl had been a chance encounter ('opportunity target' in gunnery terms) he might admit to a score (usually exaggerating) of between one (a kiss on the lips) to ten. Bonus points can also be added in unusual circumstances. No record is kept, and indeed those who admit to least points are often the largest operators.

For those luckless men whose evenings show no promise, there is always the lure of various Mayfair or Soho establishments where those tired and emotional can become more tired and emotional, and the frustrated can, after certain financial discussions, have their frustration alleviated.

Off-duty life is not all venal however. Both soldiers and their officers can indulge themselves, with heavy subsidies, in playing polo at Windsor, hunting in Leicestershire, sailing on the Guards' yacht *Gladeye* or skiing at the Guards' hut at Rothiemurchus in Scotland.

PLEASURES

DRESSING UP

People dress up for costume balls and parties with a passion not seen in London, I think, since the thirties. The dazzling theatrical effect of 'authentically' dressed revellers in glorious rooms and gardens needs a huge amount of behind-the-scenes effort. Consequently costume parties go in fatiguing waves of emotional supply and demand. Four in one week (as happened in 1985) is too much ('it was in a Chelsea square but it was raining and I thought, can I really be bothered pulling out all the Georgian stuff again?') But after a spell of going out in modern evening clothes, all eyes are again fixed on the next big chance to dress up.

Costume balls and parties can be on a huge or intimate scale, but the impulse to really take trouble with every detail is vital to the success of them all. Thanks to postwar art education (art history is a 'new' academic subject imported from Germany and Switzerland in the thirties) young people are now rather visually sophisticated. They tackle dressing up with the strange hybrid avidity of scholars *and* partygoers. The date and time on an invitation, for example, says not only 'when' but *when*, meaning 1740? 1780? 1800? 1830? (v. hard to do really well), 1850? Recipients turn an invitation over in their hands and think round it for subtle clues as to what their historical demeanour should be.

The building a party is to be held in is usually a strong hint. The mood of the big Victorian Society Ball at the Reform Club in 1984 was, for me, quite clearly the 1840s. Charles Barry's wide opulent spaces (banked with white flowers) and the famous romantic staircases melting into enormous rounded mirrors, demand to be filled with an undulating sea of pastel-coloured crinolines plus spaniel-ear hair – the 'Winterhalter Look'. The Reform Club again provided the richly subdued backdrop for the Winterhalter Ball in December 1987.

'The spirit of the place' really should set the mood of a costume party. At a small non-costume concert at Lancaster House last year, the sheer conviviality of the building caused spontaneous dancing to break out. As the mid-nineteenth-century town house of the Sutherlands, Lancaster House was once the place for aristocratic assemblies to see such performers as Chopin himself and the great tragedienne, Rachel ('I come from my house to your palace,' said the young Queen Victoria). It would be another rather nice place to give a Winterhalter Ball because nowadays it seems sadly under-used for anything except the dreariest government entertaining.

So far (we have two years to go) the most significant costume ball of the decade was the Georgian Rout at Somerset House in 1985. The English invariably look perfectly natural in eighteenth-century dress — because it was Our High Moment I suppose. Some people rolled down to the Strand in real carriages but most went in black convoys of taxis ordered by the hostesses of pre-ball dinners. People who went as pre-Revolutionary French visitors had such tall hair they had to kneel on the floor of their vehicles, just as the French themselves once had to do. A few other guests either had, or rigged up, sedan chairs and were galloped down to Somerset House by obliging friends. Link boys, glad to earn a modern fiver each, ran ahead. On arrival at Somerset House, guests were met by *Ipi Tombi* survivors standing about on the stairs as rather glamorous Equity blackamoors. All this sounds perfectly mad but it seemed imperative at the time.

Like all really good parties, the Rout had a Deeper Significance if you looked for it. That evening I drove through Mecklenburgh Square and down the long stretch of Doughty Street dressed as Gainsborough's portrait of Mrs Siddons. I felt London gently turn on its axis. For me the Rout symbolised something I was already writing about — the commercial pull eastwards, back to 'old' or 'Georgian' London. From then onwards, London east of Charing Cross would develop and expand, drawn by speculation in the City and Docklands.

For serious dressing-up parties, the most important person in London is Jean, the historical hair lady at Simon Wig Creations in Old Burlington Street. The old theatrical idea that if you hair is the right shape the rest of you will historically scrape through is perfectly correct. *Your head determines your historical silhouette.*

After you have browsed through some back-numbers of *Screen International*, Jean takes you to a little room with a lowered egg-box ceiling, chairs with sixties' metal legs ending in lipstick-stub feet, a tremendous number of mirrors and on the wall two rather debased rococo brackets enhanced with squiggles like Bird's Dream Topping. On the dressing-table before you is a glorious tangle of resting hairpieces, ashtrays with cig ends (theatricals still smoke), bottles of acetone, hairpins, empty Anadin packets, more oval hand mirrors and aerosol cans of German theatrical colour spray ('to be sprayed on hair from a not too near distance').

Jean always carries a huge rare book full of minuscule and rather dreadful drawings called *Fashions in Hair – The First 5,000 Years* by Richard Corson (Peter Owen, 1965). Since the dawn of time women's hairstyles have changed every six months and this marvellous book not only charts all this but sub-divides it into day, evening, fashionable, conservative, individual, eccentric, nationality, and rank. Luckily, as I was Mrs Siddons on this occasion, the loose, insouciantly curled English hair of the 1780s was a fairly self-evident choice. Theatrical colour sprays are too harsh for social use, so I said I would powder the hair myself with Boots' fuller's earth to give a soft painterly effect. The trial three-foot long hairpiece was then whisked upstairs like a fox's brush to be put on a block and curled by an historical wig dresser.

When it comes to clothes, girls from rather grand families often have a genuine shredded eighteenth-century dress or bodice which Mummy found in an attic. Many other girls who go to dressing-up parties regularly have genuine eighteenth- or nineteenth-century shoes, Georgian paste buckles, silk flowers (French are best), gloves, cloaks, beaded bags, jewellery or bits of lace. But again, the silhouette beneath it is vital. Even if it is only to hire stays, busks, panniers, hip rolls or crinoline cages, a trip to Bermans & Nathans (Europe's leading theatrical costumier) is usually vital. Bermans & Nathans' production stock is housed on vast floors of a wonderful red-brick warehouse in Camden Town. Every year its quietly scholarly staff dress thousands of people for the world's historical film and TV industry. Then they unpack the garment, mend it, clean it, iron it or just make it all over again.

All this can mean then that partygoers can run into patches of showbiz difficulty. An evening dress for a Regency supper? 'Sorry, all the best 1800 dresses are out for the TV remake of *Emma*.' A simple sprigged cotton day-dress of 1740? 'We've just done 2,000 extras for *Revolution*.' An 1820s dress for a Beidermeyer Ball? 'You won't believe this, but all the nicest dresses in size twelve have gone to *Papillon* (the love story of Schumann and Clara Weick).

It is always at this point that you have twenty-four hours to shop and cook dinner for twenty-five, book the baby-sitter, send your husband with a chit to Distillery Lane, Hammersmith, to collect three bags of dry ice for the machine *you know* will produce a wonderful effect of mist rolling down the stairs, pray your rich friend in Eaton Terrace will send her son round with a bag of silver candlesticks to lend a glint to your plebian quarters and pour yourself an enormous gin. People who dress up don't really want to live in the past (*no, thank you*) but like the inspired chaos of the theatre itself, suddenly it all works and for another evening – you're on!

DRESSING DOWN

Striptease in London is on the whole stupefyingly stale.

We have no real equivalent of the Lido or the Folies Bergère. Our most upmarket and lavish 'erotic' spectacle is Paul Raymond's Revue Bar. Mr Raymond spends money on his lights and costumes and props and genitals attached to slim young legs but he's not good at finding girls who can act or dance.

The show looks like a modelling class for fifth formers in Southend-on-Sea. One small blonde girl bounced around the stage with the friendly gaucherie of a four-year-old in Mom's makeup and high heels. She was dressed as a glamour queen who for some reason was doing kicks over her sceptre and when she occasionally missed, her smile was disarming – a refreshing change from the sullen posing that everyone else was doing. She was the only glimmer of ingenuousness and warmth during the entire two-hour performance.

Mr Raymond's show on a *Spy* visit was throbbing with disco beat, motorcycles, racing cars, strobe lights, and wind fans, and almost completely without personality and wit. In one scenario three semi-nude girls studiously try to untangle their ropes, chains and whips while they gyrate out of time to the climax of Carl Orff's *Carmina Burana*. It could have been funny except that no one on the stage let us know that they found it the least bit silly. If you laughed, you'd have been laughing at it not with it. But the show is certainly for some. If your cup of tea is fantasising about having sex with mannequins who move with the rhythmic variety and subtlety of clothes in a spin-dryer, then it's for you. The Japanese seem to like that kind of thing if the fact that they make up most of Mr Raymond's audience says anything. Or maybe they've just got better expense accounts.

The next rung of the ladder is the Mayfair club circuit.

They're scattered around Jermyn Street and Bond Street and are not only dull but expensive. The waiters, the muzak makers, the hostesses and the strippers appear to be straining to stay awake. But watch out, on issues of money they have the singlemindedness of the proverbial shark. There's passion a'plenty in those places, reserved entirely for the contents of your wallet. The clientele are generally drunk, overfed, middle-aged, public school boys and their business colleagues from abroad. If the shoe fits, wear it. You might feel at home in the atmosphere.

Each of these clubs has the same strip acts – about fifteen women walk from club to club. The women are slimmer, taller and better-dressed than the ones who work the lower echelons of London striptease. Several are ex-West-End chorus girls who dance to a professional standard but the problem is the same, frozen grimaces instead of smiles and deadness in the eyes. One exception – a sex change named Roxie who's been on the scene for donkey's years and who occasionally lights up places with a big bold Mae West wit and vah-vah-vah-voom. In form she can change the atmosphere from that of an animated mortuary into a semblance of a good time. She can be delightful and very funny.

The next rung of the strip ladder, the Soho clubs, are a dying breed. There are only two left, the Sunset Strip (Dean Street) and the Carnival (Old Compton Street) – four, if you count a couple of after-hours' drinking clubs, Jack's and the Capricorn (Goodge Street). The clubs themselves are seedy basements where the paint is peeling and things are not as clean as they might be. But they are much easier on the pocket than Mr Raymond or the Mayfair clubs. Jack's and the Capricorn charge prices similar to a pub's and tend to be frequented by obstreperous louts out for late night drinking. They often have public-school accents and almost without exception wear suits and ties. They're not much different from the Mayfair customers, but slumming it they feel free to get even more drunk and boorish. The Carnival and the Sunset on the other hand are much more sober and egalitarian dives.

Here there are no drinks and as the man says at the door no hidden extras – you pay your £4 and that's it. Both audience and performers are an eclectic lot – from ancient tramps to teenaged fashion models and every conceivable permutation between. There's nothing airbrushed about this place. There's even a punter who wears just a girdle and high heels. Sometimes you get batches of young fellows from Newcastle or Birmingham decked out in black and white or blue. When there's a fresh-faced out-of-town bunch that aren't too drunk the place can liven up considerably. The women on stage are only human. They respond to a bit of genuine bonhomie with genuine bonhomie, but for the most part their eyes are a mirror reflection of the eyes watching them – as cold and stony as a reptile's. They make less effort to cover up whatever they might happen to be feeling than do the Mayfair performers. After all they get paid a lot less, with a few exceptions.

Tracy is paid double what the other girls get. She's so popular that when she does turn up (she's been semi-retired for years) a sign appears outside the door at the Sunset Strip saying 'Tracy'. Business then doubles. The secret of her allure is not in a more graphic gynaecological display than the others – it would be hard to exceed some of them on that score – but in a sort of relaxed motherly condescension. She is well into her forties, has children and grandchildren, she sags everywhere and can't dance, but she still packs them in. She works on the premise that men are silly little fellows and if you can do the tired old tricks, like lick their ties and blow on their glasses without scowling at them for being so ridiculous then they will be pleased as punch and will offer to pay you twenty times what you paid for underwear at Marks & Spencer. She has made a lot of money by capitalising on this understanding of the male psyche. She'll tell you that they're pathetic, but she knows how to smile at them as though she means it. Unfortunately these days she limits herself to rare guest appearances.

Finally there are the strip pubs. They're scattered all over London although they're probably thickest around the East

End and run the gamut from upmarket and plush to places reeking of last night's vomit. The women who strip in them also cover a wide spectrum, from a few classy performers of the Mayfair club variety to women with varicose veins and cellulite thighs. As usual neither what they look like nor how explicit they are says much about their ability to keep a pub's attention. Blue, Candy and Lynne (none of them young girls) know how to make themselves the centre of attention. Each of them has a sense of rhythm and a warmth that makes them very watchable. Unfortunately most of the women who strip in pubs are eminently ignorable and everyone ignores them.

The women are sent to the pubs by a couple of agencies and even they don't know who'll they'll send where until the morning in question. As good a bet as any are the Queen Anne in Vauxhall Walk and the Lord Nelson in Mora Street, near the City. They are both reasonably comfortable places that show six girls a day, seven days a week. It's the luck of the draw.

Whether you go to Mayfair or Soho or deepest Hackney for striptease, what you're likely to find is a bored, sour-faced girl dancing for a bored, sour-faced crowd. Once in a blue moon the girl is talented enough to turn the tide and just as occasionally the crowd is friendly and in high spirits and the girl picks up on it. Even in jaded old London striptease isn't always a sordid bore. Happen on the right place at the right time and it can be a lot of fun.

About The Lord's Business

At Lord's you might think, on a summer's day,
that the actual Angels of the Lord were all at play –
those great superhuman figures in brilliant white
are truly a most divine and celestial sight.
It's all a ritual, and we are the congregation,
as we surround them with due applause and admiration.

SPECTATOR SPORT

One of the greatest moments in sport is the Saturday noon rendezvous behind the parapet on the south terrace at Twickenham where that distinguished band of rugby supporters known as 'Uncle Monty's Own' gather twice a year for England's games in the Five Nation Championship. Uncle Monty passed on some years ago and towards the end the old gentleman was so blind that it was doubtful whether he could even see as far as the touchline. Mind you, even in the days when he had eyes like a buzzard's he couldn't see much by kick off on account of the prodigious amount of alcohol he had sunk. His surviving friends still talk with awe of the day he was sick over the Welsh a few minutes before the National Anthem. The crowd was so wedged that his victims, stranded on the steps below the edge of the parapet, were unable to wreak any revenge but just had to stand there wiping their hair and cursing. They couldn't see the game either. Another time Uncle Monty kicked a beer can at a copper after yet another England loss. He was over seventy at the time. It's on account of elderly hooligans like him that the Rugby Football Union has become so tough about not allowing bottles into the ground.

The meetings of 'Uncle Monty's Own' are more decorous now that he has departed. The other founding members are getting longer in the tooth and less blessed in the bladder, but the picnics are still great feasts. Indeed the gourmandising has become increasingly competitive as more members have been admitted. On a good day there may be as many as thirty though sometimes the tickets have been so tricky to get that as few as three or four have kept the colours flying. You have to get there as soon as the gates open at noon to be sure of bagging the regular spot. And as kick off is sometimes not until three there is plenty of time for a party. Jeanette, the Chinese GP from Saracens, brings a whole salami; Allison, the mature student who has only been once and almost froze to death, sends quiches and samosas with her husband and her daughter Emma, who is almost as knowledgeable and enthusiastic as Jeanette; Philip and Myrtle, who is Uncle Monty's niece, bring a proper wicker hamper with pheasant and consommé and baguettes; Marcel always comes with a box of éclairs; John, the burly ex-military policeman who was once attacked during the Irish game by a Paddy with an umbrella, smuggles in some very decent claret; the headmaster of Huish Episcopi Primary, a vegetarian with a ginger beard, has become famous for his wife's sticky chocolate cake. At the French match a French wife is inclined to put the Brits to shame with one of those sensational glazed apple tarts.

Standing tickets are now £3.50 and no member of the team would dream of having a seat for a home international. There was a tremendous sense of outrage when, a few years ago, the much-derided Rugby Football Union erected a new canti-levered stand in place of the old all-standing south terrace. This not only reduced the amount of space for proper fans prepared to stand but also increased the number of boxes and debentures which tend to be taken up by the clients of advertising agencies who, in the eyes of the UMO, should not even be allowed in the ground. There was a time when you could buy tickets from Keith Prowse or the RFU itself but those days are long since gone. The best way is to belong to a rugger club some way from London where members are not interested in entering the ballot for tickets.

The rather insane thing is not that tickets for the inter-nationals are so hard to come by, but that for a top class club match that same ground, which holds around 60,000 will contain no more than a few hundred serious spectators. In January 1987 there were 5,000 *aficionados* for the final England trial and the rugby correspondents thought it a surprisingly high turnout. Its all those account executives with their wretched debentures.

The southwest is home to practically all the first-class London rugby clubs with only Saracens (northeast), Blackheath (southeast) and Wasps (northwest) playing elsewhere. Facilities are usually rudimentary – one fairly shabby stand and a clubhouse with bar, but the atmosphere is convivial though it may offend those who can't stand duffel coats and Old Bruno pipe tobacco. At £2 a ticket for the chance to see some of the best teams in Britain it's extraordinary value.

Soccer is a different matter. There does seem to be less serious crowd violence but even a fairly tame-sounding game like Queen's Park Rangers and Sheffield Wednesday attracts police – cavalry and infantry – in a quantity which is bleakly depressing even if you don't find it downright intimidating. And even in the affluence of £8 or £9 seats you are lucky to escape the tattooed obscenities of the yob society baying for broken bones. You could argue that they were just Uncle Monty without the privilege but it wouldn't be convincing. That sort of soccer fan exudes real hatred. Nor is it only the traditionalist who finds the modern plethora of London sides in the first division absurd. Tottenham Hotspur, Arsenal and Chelsea are authentic First Division sides – though their stadia are distinctly scruffy – but Wimbledon, which won promotion to the first in 1986, belongs permanently in the old Third Division South. It makes no sense for clubs like Manchester United and Liverpool to play at Plough Lane, Wimbledon. Charlton Athletic who also won their way back after a prolonged absence did so in the year that they abandoned their much-loved ground, The Valley, and they now share a home with Crystal Palace at Selhurst Park. Ridiculous.

The soccer season seems to get longer and longer though this is probably the sort of middle-aged illusion which makes one amazed at the youthfulness of policemen. Conversely, the cricket season seems to get shorter. However, for anyone with time to spare, a sunny day at Lord's is still one of the great London experiences. The debenture/executive box syndrome has taken hold here, too, and there is a highly commercial aspect to the new, Getty-financed, Mound Stand. The public is also inclined to rattiness about the privileges accorded to the 13,000 or so members of the Marylebone Cricket Club. (They're allowed into the ground and pavilion every day at no charge other than their annual subscription, even during Test matches and the big knock-out cup finals.)

Nevertheless and notwithstanding, Lord's is the most famous cricket ground in the world and an extraordinarily spacious, leafy arena to find in the middle of a great city. To stand outside the Tavern with a pint of beer and watch the likes of Botham and Richards is still a rare treat. It's even rather jolly to go along for an oddity like MCC versus Ireland if you have a sense of tradition, occasion and the absurd. There probably won't be more than another hundred eccentrics in the ground.

Before they abolished the distinction between amateurs and professionals there was a regular fixture between the Gentlemen and the Players. The Oval, at Vauxhall under the shadows of the famous gasholders, is a Players' place. It lacks the majesty of Lord's but also the stuffiness which even its most ardent admirer has to concede. If Surrey has a good team – they've not been as good as Middlesex in the eighties – then the Oval is a good place to be. And it is the traditional venue for the final Test.

For anyone who likes the idea of cricket as a theatrical event there are innumerable beautiful and famous club grounds: the Honourable Artillery Company off the City Road; the Duke of York's in Chelsea; Kew Green. For the Londoner who wonders if there is still an England few sights are more reassuring, as he grapples with the awfulness of the South Circular Road at the end of a weekend in the country, than that of the cricketers at Kew. It may be raining; it may be almost dark; but still out there, 'the run stealers flicker to and fro, to and fro: Oh my Hornby and my Barlow long ago.'

THE DOGS

Down by the dog track on a wet December night the crowd is muffled, huddled together against the rain, which blows in great drifts off the track, hitting them in the face like sea spray. These are the serious racegoers, disdaining the warmth of the grandstand or restaurant they accept the weather as they accept winning and losing – almost without comment, settling deeper into donkey jackets and overcoats. Most of the faces, like the shoulders, have a square, defiant set. They are city faces, pale under the arc lights, pale under any light, not exactly unhealthy but not on more than nodding terms with health either.

Over the tannoy a refined voice announces that 'the hare is running, ladies and gentlemen, the hare is running'. Against the rails the bookies, under vast umbrellas, are ostentatiously indifferent to the race, as the spectators start to lean and sway into the wind following the greyhounds round the track. The far side of the brilliantly lit course is completely dark and the shouts of encouragement and volleys of abuse are muted and carried away instantly into the huge empty space of the Wimbledon Stadium, for greyhound racing is a sport in decline.

Tracks that were built on the edge of towns and cities in the 1920s and '30s have found themselves, as the towns spread, on valuable building land, and a great tide of shopping trolleys and enterprise zones has washed over them. Of the many vanished tracks the greatest was White City and any newcomer to dog racing nowadays cannot escape hearing it endlessly and affectionately recalled. Greyhound racing is still the second most popular spectator sport in this country, but it is nonetheless the poor relation of the most popular, football, in whose premises it is now often forced to take up inferior lodgings.

Also, being a traditional English sport, it suffers from traditional English snobbery and is inclined to look down on itself. Promoters talk enthusiastically about 'getting rid of the cloth-cap image' which is neither easy – without imposing stricter dress regulations than the royal enclosure at Ascot – nor sensible. The French don't despise the beret. There has always been the aristocratic dog fancier – HRH the Duke of Kent has raced a dog which, as his trainer David Kinchett says with characteristic sang-froid, 'does give you the better sort of name' – and the story is told of a younger son who took his Glaswegian bookie home for the weekend, put him in a kilt and passed him off as the Earl of Hamilton. But greyhound racing remains a working-class sport and needs better, purpose-built tracks, not a better image.

My visits to the races are made with my friend Pudgy who, if he was not born on a greyhound track was certainly carried to one at an early age and has spent more time there since than is, strictly speaking, good for him. Pudgy knows everything there is to know about dogs – except which one is going to win – but he has the unfading optimism of the gambler. A slender man, whose shirts nevertheless always seem slightly too small for him, the combination of hope and straining buttons makes him appear ready to burst with confidence as he strides back from the bar with a fistful of pints to plan the evening's betting. Patient with my ignorance and generous with tips, Pudgy even stood by me the time I shouted for the wrong dog and couldn't understand why we hadn't won.

Greyhound racing is not generally chauvinistic, although Pudgy's claim that it is 'an equal opportunity sport' is extravagant. At Wimbledon and Wembley women become more plentiful as you move up the stadium. At the top, in the restaurant, about half the crowd is female. Raked tables allow them to watch the racing as they eat, from behind glass, as if inside a huge fish tank and the bets are placed by the waitresses. Serious punters of both sexes regard this as flippant and glare stonily from the front of the grandstand as the trays of prawn cocktail go by. Men trapped at the dinner table can sometimes be seen signalling in tick-tack through the glass to their bookies down on the track, anxious to show that they are real racegoers just giving the wife a night out.

Down in the bar there are fewer women, though all are dressed in ways that could be described as 'up'. Some are owners and owners' wives and at the end of any race involving a trophy one of them will pick her way out on to the track to be photographed clutching a cellophane-wrapped bouquet and patting the dog. With them, between races, is the occasional lady trainer, blonde and burly, favouring eager acquaintances with a curt nod. Then there is the female *hoi polloi*: barely distinguishable from their male counterparts as they troop in from the track to catch the video replay, ageless and un-made-up they stand squatly at the bar, fags a-wobble, like Oxo cubes in anoraks.

Pudgy prefers to stay at bar level and with two of his friends regularly makes up a syndicate to do the jackpot, which means backing the winner in six consecutive races. In his more detached moments Pudgy will admit that this is 'about as easy as swimming the Channel backwards underwater with your head in a biscuit tin.' However, it has been done and on that occasion the syndicate so far forgot themselves as to perform a slow waltz the length of the grandstand, thus exciting considerable comment. Under normal circumstances the mood of the dog track is one of heroic understatement. There is little heavy drinking, and discussion as the replay is shown is like an amiable Rob Wilton monologue:

'It did.'

'It didn't.'

'It did . . .'

'It never.'

'You can bloody *see* it did!'

'Did it?'

'Yeah.'

'Well . . .'

This is not to say that no one has ever been seen praying to the mosaic portrait of the legendary dog Minky Miller, set in the floor outside the gents at Wimbledon, it is just that it is not lucky to pay too much attention to that sort of thing. Once in the grandstand I was next to a man losing badly. 'Shit,' he shouted as the race ended. 'Bastard!' He banged his head on the rail hard, tore his programme in half and ran off. Pudgy, raising his eyebrows and lowering the corners of his mouth stared after him. 'Terrible,' he commented, 'People lose everything, cars, houses the lot. Terrible.' And there was a sympathetic pause before we went back to the bar to pick dogs for the next race.

Though undemonstrative himself, when his friends are winning, Pudgy, with amused indulgence, points out that 'they're going like tuning forks'. Even the most experienced will quiver with forklike concentration during a good race. Reg Potter, greyhound correspondent of *Sporting Life*, grey-haired and round-faced, clutching his programme in both hands, blinks through his spectacles with undiminished interest after forty years at the track. Years ago he worked in a bank but one visit to the dogs changed all that: 'I had three months' salary on Popeye the Sailor,' he recalls, the memory still poignant. If the syndicate loses, there is a deep silence followed by an exchange along the lines of: 'Well, this is what happens when your luck's out.' 'Yup. One of life's imponderables . . . all down to luck.'

Pudgy and his syndicate are not systems betters and believe in studying form, which is more evocatively written for dog than for horse racing. Terms vary from the hyperbolic 'every chance', implying that the dog's failure to win its last race beggars the power of human comprehension, to the pathetically honest 'knocked over'. Bets go by the usual names – monkey, pony and so forth – the latest coinage, in honour of the former deputy chairman of the Conservative party being an Archer, for a £2,000 stake. As well as past form, colour is significant and there is a prejudice against blue dogs ('piece of cheese on legs') and 'painted' or highly-marked dogs ('cheap wallpaper'). Names matter much less, though since they have to be approved, and any form of censorship is by way of being a challenge to the ingenuity of the censored, names that get through, like Ruthicman (R-U-Thick-Man?) are admired.

Beyond that it really is all down to luck. Cheating – elastic bands round dogs' toes, weighted jackets and dope – is largely a thing of the past, though at the unlicensed 'flapper' tracks literally anything goes, including terriers, sheepdogs, the same greyhound under six different names and, at one time, cheetahs. These were dropped when it was discovered they could not turn corners. Dogs on the licensed tracks are well looked after and it is affection as well as the money involved (upwards of £60,000 for a champion) that makes owner, trainer, vet and kennel maid gather round like a herd of anxious relatives if there is a problem. Though the delicacy of their legs makes greyhounds vulnerable to fractures, accidents are often less serious than they appear and a dog that has been stunned on the rails will often come round, look confusedly for the rest of the field and then trot off, unaided if disconsolate.

At the end of the evening many punters leave in a similar state. As we pick our way across the potholed car park, in itself one of the major hazards of racing, conversations drift by in the dark.

'That's it. I'm through.'

'Tenner for every time you've said that?'

'Wish I had.'

'Fiver says you're back next week.'

'Get off.'

On bad nights Pudgy has had to walk home. On good ones there's enough for the Chinese restaurant and a taxi. Anyway he'll go back. Win and you want to, lose and you have to. There is – as he says – absolutely nothing better than winning, especially on the last race. 'You just collect your money and you walk out, and that is the best feeling you're ever going to get.'

LUNCH

'Eia age! aliquis prandio?' The cry was familiar in London, even in Roman days. 'I say, anyone for lunch?' and the preppy centurions would go charging off to their favourite eating-place on the banks of the Thames, close to what is now Dolphin Square. (Indeed, there is today a restaurant close to that site, Villa dei Cesari, where the menu is still written in Latin – 'grillae', 'legunorum', and a daily 'suggestionorum angelorum.')

Beef was the Romans' most popular meat, closely followed by pork. They liked oysters for lunch, and there is not a Roman villa in the country that hasn't provided evidence of that fact. Their wine came from Italy, their olive oil and fish sauce from Spain.

In his *Descriptio Londiniae* William FitzStephen – a sort of twelfth-century Jonathan Meades – praised yet another Thames-side restaurant. 'There every day ye may call for any dish of meat, roast, fried, or sodden; fish both small and great; ordinary flesh for the poorer sort, and more dainty for the rich, as venison and fowl.' He specially recommended the goose, the 'fowl of Africa' and 'rare gadwit of Iona'.

'Lunch' was originally a variant of 'lump', meaning a piece of bread, and only gradually did it develop into boars'-heads-decorated-with-flowers, and roasted-peacocks-with-gilded-feet – before its sad decline into the ploughman's quiche now being served by a pub in Shaftesbury Avenue.

Highly spiced food was popular with our London fore-fathers – but they did find it expensive: ginger, galingale, cloves, cinnamon, and mace were all the feudal rage, but the average London luncher was uncertain as to where these spices came from – it was popularly supposed, for example, that cinnamon was found in phoenix' nests.

'Come to lunch!' But when? 'Lunchtime' in London could mean any time of the day. Under Henry VII, the English Court lunched at eleven o'clock in the morning – a time considered shockingly late by the French Court. Gradually, over the years, the time of luncheon got later and later – until 1740, when Pope complained vociferously that Lady Suffolk lunched as late as four o'clock in the afternoon. The rot eventually spread to the provinces: in 1805 those Oxford colleges which lunched at three began to eat at four, while those that ate at four began to eat at five.

By the time of Waterloo, six o'clock had become the fashionable time to eat – and the distinction between luncheon and dinner started to become somewhat blurred. 'I am not aware,' De Quincey wrote, 'of any man habitually dining at ten except in that classical case recorded by Mr Joseph Miller, of an Irishman who must have dined much later than ten, because his servant protested, when others were enforcing the dignity of their masters by the lateness of their dinner-hours, that *his* master invariably dined "tomorrow".'

Earlier, the smart London set pretended to like 'informal' lunches. King Henry VIII, for example, would often drop in on Cardinal Wolsey at the very last moment, accompanied by dozens of masked courtiers and a band of sixteen torchbearers with attendant drummers. 'And at his coming, and before he came into the hall, ye shall understand that he came by water to the water gate, without any noise; where, against his coming, were charged many chambers, and at his landing they were all shot off, which made such a rumble in the air, that it was like thunder.' On hearing this appalling din, His Eminence would have to put down his gin and tonic and pretend to be thoroughly surprised and ask the Lord Chamberlain 'to look what this sudden shot should mean, as though he knew nothing of the matter.'

Besides upsetting the seating arrangements, the service at such lunches could be a little erratic. 'The Duke of Newcastle gave a great dinner to his colleagues. The servants, as was customary at this period, all got drunk.'

Not that the servants' behaviour improved much over the years: in his *Life of Dr Johnson*, Boswell recalls how at the home of one literary lady of rank, 'the footman took the sugar in his fingers and threw it in my coffee . . . the spout of the teapot did not pour freely; she bade the footman blow into it.' Queen Victoria, too, suffered from bad service at the luncheon table. 'We are abominably served just now,' wrote one lady-in-waiting. 'The footmen smell of whisky and are never prompt to answer the bell and although they do not speak rudely, they stare in such a supercilious way. As for the Queen's dinner it is more like a badly arranged picnic.'

Sometimes it was the chef who caused the difficulties, especially in the eighteenth century when they could become quite carried away by their elaborate lunchtime creations. 'It is known,' wrote Horace Walpole, 'that a celebrated confectioner complained that, after having prepared a middle dish of Gods and Goddesses, eighteen-feet high, his Lord would not cause the ceiling of his parlour to be demolished to facilitate their entrée.'

Things had calmed down a bit by the nineteenth century, and it was all very scientific. At the Reform Club M. Alexis Soyer cooked amidst a veritable engine-house of steam pulleys and wheels which were used to deliver food to members in the dining room.

Meanwhile, in the City of London, workers lunched in the public dining-rooms, boiled-beef shops, chophouses, or in the numerous coffee houses. In May 1840, the House of Commons directed a committee to inquire into the operation of import duties. Their report contained a number of curious details respecting these coffee houses, which had become especially popular amongst the banking community.

'I now sell about three hundredweight of cold ham and meat every week,' said one witness. 'I was first compelled to sell it by persons going to a cook's shop and buying their meat, and asking me for a plate; and I found it a matter of some little trouble without any profit. It occurred to me that I might as well cook; and I have myself now, in consequence of that, a business during the whole of the day.' His coffee was popular because 'men of this class find they can transact their afternoon's business better after coffee than after malt liquor.'

Some Londoners, nevertheless, still preferred alcohol. In the 1880s the Hon. Henry Cumming-Bruce was sued by a restaurant for not paying his luncheon bill – a bill which had been greatly inflated on account of the number of bottles of champagne that he had consumed. He'd refused to pay on the grounds that he was under twenty-one, legally an 'infant', and that the law did not allow infants to be supplied with items of luxury on credit. The jury found against him. They decided that champagne might be fairly classed as a 'necessity' for someone in his station of life.

Of course Mr Tyson, a born autocrat, would never have let things get out of control like that. He knew that in their heart of hearts Londoners, for all their 'Rule Britannia' sentiments, like to be herded. So in 1896 he established a hot-buttered toast restaurant where he enforced laws of his own making. He provided only chops, steaks, and Cumberland ham for lunch – and served them only with hot-buttered toast. Reading was not permitted, nor protracted sitting, nor smoking.

Others, too, had strange ideas about correct lunch conduct. In his book *Seventy Years of Irish Life*, W.R. Le Fanu recalls how, after one particularly pleasant luncheon, Chief Justice Doherty, who had been one of the guests, met a Mr A . . . and said to him, 'What a pleasant party we had with you last Tuesday!'

'Do you call that a pleasant party?' said A . . . 'I don't.'

'Why not?' said Doherty.

'Too much talk, too much talk; you couldn't enjoy your wine; you drank a little more than a bottle each. On Wednesday I had nine men to dinner, and they drank three bottles a man; and you'd have heard a pin drop the whole time. That's what I call a pleasant party.'

Frank Harris was an odd eater, too. Lunching at the Café

Royal he thought nothing of putting away at a sitting two large steaks, a huge cheese and a magnum of Burgundy washed down by several liqueurs. He had convinced himself that steaks were essential to his virility and once, while downing a porterhouse, turned to a nearby lady and roared: 'We do this for your sakes!' When he was a little older, in order to maintain his self-advertised potency he used to take a portable stomach pump into lunch with him.

Not, thankfully, that the days of the eccentric eater are yet over. James Lees-Milne claims that when he invited a lady to luncheon at Wiltons' she brought with her a huge sack and instructed the waiter to fill it with oyster shells for her hens.

Funny how oysters remain a constant theme in London's lunches. Now, if the oyster-eating, lunch loving Romans were to return to London today, seeking out the fashionable tribal meeting-places, where would we direct them?

No doubt we'd explain that today's centurions tend to favour the In and Out Club or the Hyde Park Hotel; our senators move off to Lockets near the Houses of Parliament (or to the Gay Hussar if they lean *ab sinistro*); the higher-paid performers from the public circuses will be hiding, *ab multitudo*, in the St James's Club or at the Garrick; publicists and orators are to be found at the Neal Street Restaurant, Langan's or at L'Etoile in Charlotte Street; the kingmakers will be at Odins, the Caprice or Aspinall's; the kings themselves will be hiding behind the Hungarian orchestra at Claridge's; visitors from Rome will be taking advice on where to go from their fellow-countrymen, the hotel- and hall-porters of Les Clefs d'Or; leading writers on the *Acta Publica* will be found either in the Savoy Grill, at discreet luncheon clubs in the more fashionable suburbs, or drinking at El Vino's – although their scouts are now out, busily skirmishing down in Wapping.

But, of course, where they would all really *like* to be for lunch is at the Connaught.

FREELOADING

Armed with a suit, a tie and a fair amount of gall you can eat, drink and be entertained entirely at someone else's expense if you know your way about town. Some of the better things in life can now truly be yours for free.

My father used to recall how, as a youth, he would don white tie and tails, put a half-bottle of champagne, some glasses and some friends in a motor car and cruise around Belgravia and Mayfair until the sound of a party was heard. Then, talking among themselves and with a glass of champagne to hand, they would boldly enter the house. 'Never a complaint – I knew perfectly well they would have invited us if they had only known us,' he said. There would even be some genuine follow-up invitations. And of course to ensure the whole operation is cost-free, as a last gesture at the party he would take an unopened champagne bottle from the pantry to start off the next day's outing.

Not that his technique can be recommended today. For a start only pop stars, livery companies, students and musicians wear white tie and far too many people employ bouncers to make this particular technique feasible.

Today a young man new to town, you can make no better start than to call up Peter Townend. Former editor of *Burke's Peerage*, latterly Society Editor of *Tatler*, Townend is a bachelor of uncertain years whose *raison d'être* is the company of well-bred (and/or wealthy) young (and old) things. He compiles what is referred to as The List, but is actually many lists. If a debutante's mum needs suitable escorts or guests for a cocktail party, Townend will – in ever such a discreet way – find them. If a youth, after years of incarceration at public school, needs a line-up of girls from which to pick a châtelaine for his 1,000 acres of Norfolk or whatever, Townend will make the appropriate introductions. Once on the merry-go-round the invitations will be self-perpetuating.

Or else try a black-tie variation on the gate-crash trick – remember that champagne glasses in the thirties were *coupes* (modelled on a breast of Marie Antoinette, so the legend goes), now they are flutes; a dry cider will sparkle convincingly in the glass and you can find a list of coming-out parties in the *Times* and in *Harper's & Queen*. The chances are that the hosts won't know half the people there, so confidence is all.

It is worthwhile finding out discreetly who are your hosts and identifying them – do try not to insult them and do not tell people that you have not been invited. Do behave with a modicum of decorum. Do assemble some small talk. Do not espouse left-wing causes – a washy liberalism will do as long as you follow the field.

If a waitress figure with a gigantic bow in her hair hoves into view, do be polite to her for she is Mrs Betty Kenward aka the diary writer 'Jennifer' of *Harper's & Queen*. Perhaps unsurprisingly 'Jennifer' does not consider herself to be a journalist; she disdains the breed.

On the morning-after, do send an elegantly brief thank-you note, with your name and address legible so that you may continue to circulate as a good fellow. Do not worry if you have tacky or no writing paper or cards: in the foyers of all decent hotels there will be presentable paper and envelopes enough.

A useful side income can be made by picking up snippets of conversation and guiding them towards the gossip columnists of the popular press (all newspapers accept transfer charge calls), all of whom are in their forties and far too tired, bored, uninterested, lazy or old to find out such things for themselves. It's worth keeping up-to-date with the names of the columnists as this will impress folk. Not that it's easy. Diary editors seem to play constant musical chairs, and even Nigel Dempster can't go on forever.

If you think you are shaky on good form, fear not. One

'The great stand-by is the publishing party.'

infamous gossip columnist has an unctuously endearing habit of calling everyone 'Sir'. Butlers don't object, neither do dukes – anyway it's correct if you are their equal and it's the proper form for Prince Philip and Charles. Never use 'Your Highness', unless you are foreign and are making a plea of dubious merit to a magistrate: they will studiously ignore the address but some say they quite like it.

If you're too old for that lark, try the journalistic junkets. There are plenty of newspapers and magazines: if you can't find one to represent, make one up. There's an ancient and shabby figure on the freeloading scene who represents a paper that few, if any, have ever seen. Yet there he is at press launches of shows, perfumes, hotels and restaurants, tucking into the fare.

For a relaxed life, being a restaurant critic is a good scam. The good news is that you can eat for free. The bad news it that invariably you will have to make conversation with a PR person, the owner or the chef. Maybe you would feel happier with fashion, consumer affairs or books. There are always plenty of launch parties for beauty products and groups needed for weekend activities.

The great stand-by is the publishing party. It is quite safe, occasionally quite good, often filled with inexorably cheap wine and plenty of that underpaid and sometimes attractive species, the 'publishing popsy'. If you can get your name on the Publishers' Publicity Circle lists you are well away. And if you can actually claim to have got a mention for any of the books, you will gain life-long contacts. Don't worry about not knowing anyone. People will assume you are the author – traditionally no one in their right mind ever speaks to authors at publishing parties – or else, if asked, explain that you are working on a book on some randomly obscure subject. Everyone will understand if you say that you're afraid you can't discuss it. Don't explain anything. You'll be fine.

Or be a travel writer. There are 'inaugural flights' all around the world – often, it seems, to places where the airline has been flying for years. The catch here is that you would not be following the wise advice once given to me by the late Lord Chandos, cabinet minister, *bon viveur* and businessman. He called me into his study and announced: 'Young man, I'll give you a bit of advice.' I hung on his every word as he added: 'Never accept an invitation outside London.' His theory was that if you weren't enjoying a party in London, you could just go home. If you were stuck in a house in the country or – worse – on a boat travelling down the Thames, you would be forced to remain there for the duration.

Then there is the late-night circuit. Claim to represent a foreign magazine wanting to write about London clubs and call up a club owner or two – there's bound to be someone who can introduce you to Peter Stringfellow. If you can get talking to the right people, you will be invited to one of the splendid bashes to celebrate any day of the year. The gaming clubs are superb hosts. Their problem is that they make masses of money and are not allowed to advertise, so the only way they can get rid of the moolah is by laying on the most extravagant feasts as promotion.

Get yourself added to the lists of some public relations companies; there's a secretary of a certain age who works in Fleet Street who turns up to everything from a ball at the Albert Hall to champagne parties at the Dorchester. She's never written a word anywhere, but she gets away with it and has a very pleasant lifestyle with the added bonus of the samples and such like that are given to her, most of which make most excellent birthday and Christmas presents.

A late, late ploy of my father's day was to take breakfast of a glass of water and a few bread rolls at the Ritz or Savoy – it seemed the management was not averse to white tie being worn at breakfast. The introduction of cover charges has put paid to that one, although hotels do still offer a wonderful service. You can meet friends in the foyer, eat their potato crisps – the better venues make their own which knock Smith's into a cocked hat – visit their elegant and well-kept lavatories, use their telephones (it's probably an idea to avoid Claridge's as they put calls through the switchboard and have a minimum charge).

However, it is as well to recall the tale of the two business-men in New York who were travelling from Wall Street to 21 for lunch. Idly they talked of this and that and the fact that everyone, no matter how humble, had a story to tell. 'Why,' one of them said, indicating a bum spied lying face down in the gutter in the Bowery, 'even he must have a story. Driver, stop the car.'

The businessman got out and with his foot turned over the tattered figure – the clothes and their occupier had obviously once seen better and more prosperous days.

'Hey, bud,' said the businessman. 'What's your story?'

The man in the gutter slowly focused bloodshot eyes and cleared a croaky throat. Eventually he spoke. When the voice came it was with the tones of a college man. 'There is,' he said, through the living fumes of rough alcohol, 'no such thing as a free lunch.'

PUBS

There is no such thing as *the* London pub. It is not like the London bus, large, red and double-deckered. There are 6,500 pubs in Greater London, a tenth of the total for the whole of Britain, and they come in all shapes, sizes and colours. It is true that in the 1970s one large London brewing company, Watney, plumped briefly for identikit pubs, all painted a violent shade of red, their names picked out in a hideous white lettering. But as Watney's beer was not highly regarded at the time, all the exercise did was to identify too closely the purveyors of sub-standard ale. The company was advised by its marketing consultants to destandardise its pubs as rapidly as possible.

London's pubs are an integral part of the history and growth of the capital. Until the turn of the century, London was a loose conglomeration of small towns and villages, each with its clutch of pubs and taverns. Many pubs still reflect those old, not quite lost communities, their names – Blacksmith's Arms, Market Tavern, Carpenter's Arms, Founder's Arms – preserving skills and trades now subsumed by modern service industries.

Britain's infamous class divisions are mirrored by pubs which still retain public and saloon bars, but most of the capital's drinking places have been transformed into more egalitarian, one-bar establishments. To enter, for example, either the Castle or the Bishop's Finger in Smithfield Market is to see a fascinating and still rare example of class cross-fertilisation, with market porters chatting amiably to archetypal City gents before going their separate ways to terraced houses and suburban villas. The Lamb in Lamb's Conduit Street, although now one room, still keeps its snob screens which in Victorian times prevented the *hoi-polloi* in the bar observing their betters in the lounge.

To single out just a few London pubs is to play the tourist game. There are many famous pubs, rightly so, but to focus on them ignores the humbler houses, straightforward, no-nonsense boozers where people gather for a quiet drink, a chat or a game of darts, rather than self-consciously playing bit parts in an historical pageant. Some of the famous pubs, though, do deserve their plaques and to visit them is to catch a glimpse of a London what would be lost but for its last, lingering taverns and inns. The George in Southwark is the only surviving galleried Elizabethan inn, with a cobbled court-yard where Shakespeare's plays are performed occasionally in summer. Inside the low beams are a reminder of how much the average Briton has grown since the times of Queen Bess.

Ye Olde Cheshire Cheese, in the suitably bibulous Wine Office Court off Fleet Street, is another ancient, beamed establishment, much frequented by Johnson, Boswell and Reynolds. It was destroyed in the Great Fire of 1666 but was rebuilt the following year. The antique charm of its many small rooms, winding stairs and splendid restaurant was caught by the poet John Davidson: 'The modern world so stiff and pale/You leave behind you when you please/For long clay pipes and great old ale/And beefsteaks in the Cheshire Cheese.'

Close by on the corner of Queen Victoria Street there is a different slice of history. The Black Friar is indeed a slice, a ribald, wedge-shaped example of turn-of-the-century art deco, designed by H. Fuller Clark and the sculptor Henry Poole. It is built on the site of a Dominican priory where the friars were more famous for their imbibing than their devotions. Mosaics and panels outside show friars welcoming customers to an interior decorated in coloured marble and with more bronze tableaux of monks.

Along the banks of the Thames are several old inns heavy with history. The Mayflower, formerly the Spreadeagle, was renamed to mark the spot where the founding fathers set sail for the Americas. The Dove at Hammersmith, built in the reign of Charles II, has been frequented over the years by a diversity of writers including William Morris (who lived next door), Ernest Hemingway and Graham Greene.

Two pubs that also stand by the Thames epitomise the conflicting attitudes to modern pub design. The Dickens Inn at St Katharine's Dock was built in the 1970s in a synthetic, plaster-and-plastic, Disneyland attempt to create an Elizabethan tavern. It will delight those who enjoy folksy charm, Stratford-upon-Avon, fast food and coffee granules. Young and Company, fiercely independent and traditionalist brewers from south London, eschewed flummery and fakery when they were granted the licence for a pub on the new Bankside Reach development. The Founder's Arms marks the spot where foundries forged the bells for St Paul's across the water. It is an unashamedly modern pub with a long bar, ample seating and separate dining area. Both the glassed front and terrace give fine views of the Thames. On a warm summer evening there is no better way to enjoy Young's bitter than to watch, as the sun goes down, the lights of St Paul's and St Bride's begin to cast shimmering reflections in the river.

The Dickens Inn and the Founder's Arms signal the crisis of identity that is worrying the devotees of the London pub scene. Brewers large and small have been concerned by the slump in beer sales in the past decade. They have spent money in making pubs more pleasant and no longer all-male, cracked lino and smelly loos. Women are now valued customers, with the emphasis on comfort and better food. In many cases, though, the changes have been too violent, too sudden, and threaten to destroy the ruminative nature of the pub.

One company, the Host Group, part of Watney-Grand Metropolitan, has revamped its outlets as a result of 'demographic studies' of the areas in which they stand. Some pubs, it has been decided, should be disco bars, all blaring music and strobe lighting, aimed at the young. Others are determinedly traditional, à la Dickens Inn, while yet more have a family and restaurant ambience. The problem with such quasi-scientific marketing is that it ignores the essential welcome-to-all nature of the pub. It may be that a majority of people in one small area may rush salivating to a darkened den pulsating to rock rhythms but it is scarcely worthy of the name 'public house' if it debars those who would prefer a quiet drink as they read their papers.

In the area near King's Cross known as the Angel (in common with many parts of London, it is named after a pub) there are some glaring examples of brewers' overkill. A pleasant old pub called the Shakespeare has been turned into a 'café-bar' called Le Dôme. The splendid Empress of Russia, close to Sadler's Well Theatre, has had its two rooms knocked into one. Piped pop has replaced the television set thoughtfully provided for older customers who watched it over a glass of Guinness. The pensioners have voted with their feet, making way for the deeper pockets of the gin-and-tonic office brigade. At least its name has been left intact. The Fox at Islington Green has not been so lucky. This Watney house has been given the ludicrous new appendage of Slug and Lettuce (surely an invitation not to eat there), its bare boards, wine by the bottle and quasi-French cuisine aimed at Felicity and Rodney Upwardly-Mobile.

The Slug and Lettuce is a half-hearted attempt by a large brewer to follow one of the recent success stories in London pubs. David Bruce, a chirpy young businessman, became disenchanted with working for national brewing firms. He thought that he could run better pubs than they do. His first outlet was a derelict ex-Truman house in a dingy side street near the Elephant and Castle. Other brewers turned the place down and scoffed when Bruce bought it. It was packed on opening day and has remained that way. The Goose and Firkin has spawned a small chains of Firkins (old English for a nine-gallon beer cask). The stress is on fun without frills: bare wooden floors, wooden seats, open fires, large helpings of plain, wholesome grub, and beer brewed in the cellar. This is a return to a genuine tradition, to a time before the rise of the brewery-owned 'tied house', when every publican was a home brewer and victualler. Bruce's bubbling enthusiasm has rubbed off on his legion of loyal customers, who wear his

T-shirts and sweaters, and take part in his fun runs and pub competitions.

Bruce's apotheosis is the Phoenix and Firkin, designed as part of British Rail's Denmark Hill station in south London. It is a symbol not only of Bruce's aggressive attitude to successful pub business but also of the innate conservatism and horror of competition that are the shabby hallmarks of the major brewing companies – the 'beerage', as they are ironically known.

When Denmark Hill station burnt down in the early 1980s, British Rail asked commuters what facilities they would like when the station was rebuilt. The majority chose a pub. The brewers were invited to tender, turned the site down and then took court action in an attempt to stop Bruce getting a licence. He won and now brewery directors grit their teeth in fury when they sup Bruce's brew in his brilliant, cavernous bar, replete with railway memorabilia.

The London pub will survive because entrepreneurs such as David Bruce will retain its essential character. The influx of regional brewers from Scotland and the north of England, who also avoid the fake and the flashy, will add their contribution to tradition and cheer. Above all, the pub will endure because pub users, the punters, will determine it, ensuring that in a capital that is often harsh and hostile there will be havens of warmth and welcome. The pub is not just part of London's history but a hopeful harbinger of its future.

WINE

What little I know about wine I picked up in the early 1970s from two of the most unlikely characters who ever bestrode the London wine scene. One was the splendid Ahmed Pochee, a teetotal Pakistani who started Oddbins by the simple expedient of leasing premises in various high streets and selling bin ends.

You had to look at the vintage years a bit carefully to make sure that the Property of a Gentleman (Deceased), bought at auction, wasn't way over the hill. And you had to ferret around among the dusty boxes of wine, unstacking them one by one to see what was at the bottom.

Suddenly, wine buying was fun. Twenty years ago, the few who bought wine went to small, stuffy wine merchants, generally staffed by a superannuated undertaker, who was usually doing the *Telegraph* crossword puzzle. I got the impression he never wanted to sell you a single bottle because he secretly intended to drink the entire stock himself.

So he parted with a bottle or two only after making it clear he was doing you a considerable favour. It would be laboriously wrapped in several layers of tissue paper, sometimes held together with a red wax seal. After that, the cheerful anarchy of Oddbins came as a breath of fresh air. And the ex-petrol pump attendants, or whoever they were behind the Oddbins counters, had their own ways of drumming up business. 'Try this one, squire, it'll put lead in your pencil' led me to my first encounter with a hearty red from the Hunter Valley in Australia and afterwards I went back for more.

The other great liberator of the 1970s was Brian Barnett, a large, bearded man in baggy trousers, who looked rather like a bell tent put up by an incompetent Scout troop. Brian

carried the Oddbins revolution a stage further. With parking
meters and double yellow lines marching up the high streets,
he looked for cheap leases on tatty shops in side streets, with
easy parking, for his Augustus Barnett chain of cash-and-carry
wine shops.

The only concession to public relations was an annual,
immensely drunken cruise down the Thames for wine writers
and top staffers to the Barnett HQ at Silvertown in London's
Docklands. You were herded aboard by a PR man with a
smile like a silent scream, who wore a bilious yellow suit that
was probably put down on his expenses sheet as 'office
redecoration'.

Watching Brian buy was a revelation. He sat beside his
phone fielding calls from the wine countries, stubby fingers
flicking over the keys of a pocket calculator to work out his
profit margin. He loved dealing with German winegrowers
because he said they were gentlemen, and deeply distrusted
the French. In the end, he over-extended himself and was
taken over by the Spanish sherry company, Rumasa, who
then went spectacularly bust.

Brian started again with another chain of wine stores called
Bottoms Up but his heart was no longer in the business. I'm
told he now sells villas in Minorca.

His great achievement was to cut the mystique and much
of the snobbery out of wine. Up till then, we had bought
seventy per cent of our wine from hotels and restaurants,
preferring to pay twice or three times the retail price of the
bottle in order to get advice from an openly contemptuous
wine waiter who sneered and snapped his cuffs in a threatening manner.

Nowadays, you can always match wine with food by reading the back labels carefully before buying. The supermarkets,
led by Sainsbury's, do a good job here and now have sixty
per cent of all off-licence sales. Sainsbury's is by far the biggest
wine merchant in the country and there are regular adulatory
choruses from the wine writers about Sainsbury's champagne,
their Chablis, their Portuguese wines, and a scattering of fine

Bordeaux, such as Château Maucaillou from the Moulis. Only their Alsace wines let them down.

I think a supermarket's primary function is as a wine library. Customers take in essential knowledge through their pores, simply by browsing among the crisply written back labels. Forearmed, the London *Spy* can then consider a glorious range of wine merchants, such as no other capital city in the world possesses.

The grandest establishments yield great treasures for those on a modest budget. And what could be grander than Berry Bros & Rudd at the bottom of St James's Street and just a matter of yards from the sentries outside St James's Palace? Founded in 1699 and renowned for its vintage ports and fine clarets, it has uneven floors and high panelled walls dark with age, and soft-voiced young men in beautiful suits, not long out of public school, to serve you.

Dare you enter this holy of holies wearing bicycle clips or a bomber jacket and orange crash helmet? You dare, because Berry Bros is the only wine merchant I know that has its own man, Gerard Casey, permanently stationed in Bordeaux to snap up unconsidered trifles from *petits châteaux*. They will point you unerringly towards unknown clarets with unrecognisable names. Their disarming Good Ordinary Claret ('Well, we've always had a Good Claret and also an Ordinary Claret, so we put the two together . . .') is about £40 a case and drunk by Top Names.

Victoria Wine are the biggest of the off-licence chains. They have 865 shops and are good for Vin de Pays (a cut above Vin de Table) from France and for the marvellous Raimat Abadia, a fragrant, fruity Spanish red from the hinterland behind Barcelona that many would mistake for honest Bordeaux at a dinner party.

For some of the best Loire and Rhône wines, you may have to go outside London to former dentist, Robin Yapp, in Mere, Wiltshire. Funny how wine and dentists go together. London dentist Howard Ripley has an extraordinarily good list of burgundies from smaller growers at reasonable prices that is the envy of many larger wine merchants. He operates from 35 Eversley Crescent, N21.

Ten years back, the best advice about Australian wines came from the Australian Wine Centre in Frith Street, bang opposite (to the horror of hairy-kneed Ozzie visitors) a male strip joint. Sadly, the wine centre has closed but its place has been taken unofficially by an Australian, Ross Sheppard of Ostlers at 63(a) Clerkenwell Road, EC1. I don't know of anyone else with such a wide-ranging selection. Sheppard is just as liberal with advice about Californian wines as Australian, which he also stocks in great profusion.

As long as you order by the case, GB Vintagers supplies Château Doisy-Védrines, a lusciously sweet Sauternes with a nice, clean finish and the zingy Loire sparkling wines of Monmousseau. I have never quite forgiven them for leaving their original cellars, which were underneath the arches below King's Cross Station, with the rumble of heavy locomotives overhead. But I still buy from them Les Rigaudes, the best Côtes du Rhône to be found anywhere in London, which has a woman in charge of the vineyards. They are now at 430 High Road, Willesden, NW10.

At 105 Old Brompton Road, SW7 you will find La Vigneronne, where Liz and Mike Berry not only have a sound, middle-brow range of wines with style and character but also stock old Madeiras and the sweet white wines of Banyuls for those with rarefied palates. However rushed they are, they invariably find time to offer dispassionate advice, even remembering to ask how you got on with a previous purchase when you come back for more. You can buy mixed cases of the top wines from Alsace from them and there's a cross Amazonian parrot in one corner, who was wished on Liz by a previous boss. The limit of his conversational powers is 'Hullo'.

A world away from the panelled tasting rooms of the St James's wine merchant are the new wine warehouses, which began opening in London in July 1982. That was when wholesale licences for the drinks trade were abolished, which means anyone can sell wine by the case from garage or garden shed to passing motorists. It's a bit like the old days of Oddbins, except for a classier kind of customer. BMWs, Porsches, supercharged Renaults and Alfa Romeos tank up on case lots of Beaujolais or Australian Rhine Reisling for jolly weekends in Maidenhead or Tunbridge Wells, though two of the early warehouses, Majestic and the Noble Grape, went bust before opening under new management.

One that I think has disappeared filled your empty bottle with draught *vin de table* from picturesque wooden casks that were in turn topped from stainless steel containers. The place was tucked away under a dank railway arch near Tower Bridge and rain dripped through the roof in a steady patter.

'People think it's so terribly rustic down here,' said the manager. 'We wouldn't be without the romance of the wine business, now would we?' Up to a point, Lord Copper, I suppose we wouldn't.

The Tate Gallery

Nobody could hate
the Tate –
or make strictures
on the pictures.

ART

Art Now in London or How to Enjoy Yourself with the London *A to Z* at the Cost of a Leg or Two but not an Arm . . . From Hackney to Portobello and points East, West, North and South.

In the early 1980s the American octogenarian and vastly distinguished painter Willem de Kooning produced some of the jolliest, creamiest, most succulent and attractive paintings of his career. Critically praised, sought by museums, the paintings were an offer in London and New York. They were displayed in those sharply lit white spaces which make up the grand shops known as art galleries for, it was rumoured, $350,000 a time.

The price is peanuts compared to old masters, impressionists, and even at auction major de Koonings, not to mention the modern masters of the marketplace from Picasso to Jasper Johns. Even some living British artists can be included in top-priced art-market stocks on sale in galleries and auction rooms. Francis Bacon, David Hockney, Howard Hodgkin, Frank Auerbach, to name but a few, all have waiting lists for much of their output. Bacon, at auction, regularly tops $1 million.

These pretty white spaces – the commercial art galleries – and the auction rooms, with their red velvet walls, are usually to be found around the centre of town. Art galleries like Agnews, Colnaghi's and the Fine Art Society, the auction houses, Sotheby's and Christie's, have been out and about in Mayfair – Bond Street and St James's – for a century or even two.

But art in London has now diversified out of the West End to points further afield. This adds to the sense of adventure and discovery. London is a series of villages and exploring from Portobello to London Fields yields an unexpected harvest of art – and living artists. Some enterprising firm should set up art safaris, for if you want to chance your eye, back your hunch with buying contemporary art at reasonable prices – one-thousandth of that established de Kooning, for instance – strike out for these old village market areas of London which, in the 1980s, are the new artists' haunts.

The postwar British vice is nostalgia: looking backwards to a past that never was. The Victorians were vigorous patrons of contemporary artists. They tore down much of London, too: more was lost to 'development' in the nineteenth century than was lost in the Blitz. Looking backwards makes it ever easier to trip over yourself as you stroll on, not to mention doing nothing for that much vaunted 'heritage' for the future. The present has as much to do with the future as the past. Anyone anyway can back somebody else's discoveries; it is certainly more instructive to make one's own. And everything of worth was after all discovered once, and mistakes are less painful because less expensive. A healthy country, and a healthy art, has to live in the present, not off the past.

Surprisingly though, the east of London – Hackney to be specific, that tubeless wilderness of bus routes and Georgian survivors in a once-blitzed landscape – now houses more artists than any area comparable in geographic extent in Europe – even America.

Around Whitechapel and Bethnal Green, tube-served districts, efforts were made in the nineteenth and early twentieth century by West Enders to bring institutionalised culture east. Notably this resulted in the Bethnal Green Museum, a building that was once on the site of, and part of, the Victoria and Albert. It was moved bodily and is thought to be one of the first metal-framed prefabricated buildings in the world. Once a cabinet of curiosities, it was much commended by Henry James, and is now the Museum of Childhood. Just after the turn of the century the Whitechapel Art Gallery was founded, and happens to be one of London's exceptionally rare art-nouveau buildings. So amidst the poverty, the waves of successive immigration that succeeded the mercantile and trading prosperity, and funded the Hawksmoor churches and Georgian terraces of earlier centuries, there were two small, potent institutionalised culture palaces, not to mention Shoreditch's Geffrye Museum created out of a terrace of seventeenth-century almshouses.

Slowly, it is all being gentrified: the echoes of 'Big Bang', the government-backed plans for transport, new industry, middle-class housing, even Sir Terence Conran's Museum for Design planned for Docklands. But the artists got there first. The witty and powerful performance artists, painters, draughtsmen and photographers, Gilbert and George have lived ritualistically for years in Spitalfields (and of course there is a Spitalfields Society and a Spitalfields Festival). It is said they eat dinner – meat and two veg – for breakfast at a local transport café. Of course, the M25, the last gasp of the national obsession with motorways (do you remember, in 1959, the 'Song of the Motorway', the M1 that was, on the radio?) may 'do' for transport cafés what the gentrification process does for struggling artists: wipe them out from their natural habitat.

The East End for artists all began in the late 1960s with the use of the magnificent Telford riverside warehouses for artists' studios at St Katharine's Dock (now the site of hotels, and commercial development). Space was an artist-initiated movement, and rapidly developed into the extraordinary common sense strategy of taking over disused buildings – warehouses, schools, hospitals, factories – on short leases with council cooperation; even councils sometimes prefer artists and art to dereliction and squatters. By the mid 1980s Space provided rented studio accommodation for over 260 artists on twenty sites in London. The demand is now so great, the artistic vitality in London so strong – never can there have been so many good artists, with so lackadaisical and indifferent a public as we have in England – that there are over 200 professional artists on the waiting list for Space studios alone.

Space does provide information on how to set up independent studios, and while artists' complexes stretch from Greenwich to Lewisham, Hammersmith to Camden, most, whether Space, Acme (an artists' housing association) or independent are situated in the East End.

London has, however, experienced the phenomenon found in many other major cities: artists as a group act as an economic and social avant-garde. Yuppies follow in the pathway that the Bohemian artists clear through the undergrowth of the city. The irony is that the trendy young professionals price out the artists who rehabilitated the neighbourhood in the first place. So go art prospecting while you can.

Regularly listed and described in the London events magazines such as *Time Out*, the specialist art magazines like *Art Monthly* and *Arts Review* and *ArtScribe*, and the free monthly magazine *Gallery*, are the openings of artists' studios which enable the punter not only to see a great deal of art, but where it is made – and by whom. Visiting artists' studios is like an indoor safari, but with luck the visitor – and potential purchaser – is not only intrigued and fascinated by something, somewhere, but gains some insight into the whole process by which the gleam in the artist's eye is translated into some tangible reality. Everyone starts somewhere: both purchaser and artist.

Another kind of agreeable and informative art safari is the visit to the art school show. Art colleges put on degree shows for graduating students, and it is here that businesses (fashion firms, textile and ceramic manufacturers, for example) go prospecting for talent. You can, too. After all, David Hockney was an art student once, his work snapped up from his showing at the Royal College of Art not only by collectors but also by art galleries.

Finally, the art hunter must seek out not just artists' studios – which still in their unheated vastness nicely conform to some notions of artistic struggle – and the young, ambitious student in the lair of the art college, but also the up-and-coming gallery districts. Currently, the newest and most enterprising area in London is Portobello, long the home of antiques and old clothes, it is now designer trendy. The comparatively low rents and the neighbourliness of it all have attracted so many art galleries – nearly a dozen at last count – that the first Portobello Art Festival was held in April 1987. The wine was vile, the company wonderful, and the artists and their art, young, new and up-coming – the names of the future – waiting to be discovered.

And, by the way, the Contemporary Art Society, c/o the Tate Gallery, 20 John Islip Street, London SW1, runs courses for art collectors, and art safaris. So you can chance your luck on a guided tour.

Shaftesbury Avenue

In the States
you don't get Theater
at such fantastically low rates.

THEATRE

Such is the innate puritanism of the British that in the English theatre one law at least is generally in force: the higher the artistic aspirations, the lower the standard of comfort. In the case of some of the best of the fringe theatres, the fact that the auditoria are small, murky rooms above pubs may excuse the inconvenience of being obliged to sit on other people's feet and to have other people sit on one's own. But in the case of the Pit, which is part of the Barbican, and of the Cottesloe, which is part of the National Theatre, it is difficult to see why the distinguished architects, so lavish of their expenditure in most other respects, could not have provided seating accommodation at least of the standard of a second-class railway carriage.

Perhaps it is in the belief that art and arithmetic are incompatible, even hostile to each other, that so often in 'studio' theatres there is no numbering of seats. As an adolescent 'theatre-fan' (as we called ourselves in prewar days) I would frequently queue for gallery or pit. But at least my fellow-queuers and I could put down stools, and there were always jolly, if not always talented, buskers to entertain us. At these modern theatres, however, the disconsolate queuers have to stand, and the only entertainment is provided by the admittedly sometimes mirth-provoking conversations of the people in front or behind. Once everyone has filed in, politely exasperated or, on some occasions, shrilly indignant exchanges can be heard. 'Yes, I'm keeping all seven of those seats, I'm afraid.' 'Yes, I have some friends arriving any moment now.' 'I put my *Guardian* there, just there, while I slipped out for a moment to see if I could buy a copy of the text.' 'Excuse me, I most certainly *was* in the queue. Anyone might have to obey a call of nature on an evening as cold as this.'

Commercial managements do not deliberately create

discomfort and inconvenience in this fashion – indeed, it was edifying to see how, as soon as Ian Albery had taken over the Donmar Warehouse from the RSC, the seats were at once renewed and numbered and a bar was installed (before that members of the audience would scuttle out to the nearest pub in the interval, some of them never to return) – but often outdated design and the ravages of time conspire to do so hardly less effectively. Everyone would agree that the Theatre Royal in the Haymarket is one of the most elegant of London theatres; but during a shaky performance by Peter O'Toole in *Man and Superman* I was equally shaky on my aisle seat, balancing on it as though on a shooting-stick at a point-to-point. The foyers and passageways of our Victorian and Edwardian theatres are so restricted that one can only suppose that, when they were built, audiences did not have to think of anything so vulgar as last trains or babysitters. The perfect London theatre is, to my mind, the Lyric at Hammersmith. Here an elegantly ornate Edwardian theatre, once standing elsewhere in the same area, has been lovingly rebuilt inside a concrete shell which allows ample space for coming in and going out, for frequenting bars and restaurant, or just for sitting at one's ease.

The 'Crush Bar' of the average theatre is all too aptly named. I wish that all theatre bars would adopt the practice, pioneered by a few, of having glasses of red and white wine, already poured, set out for sale in the interval. This would preserve one from the man in a dinner-jacket with a pleated mauve shirt and cuff-links the size of bar-bells, who cheerfully elbows one aside to shout to the barmaid: 'Three double gins with tonic, love. Oh, and a Campari soda. No make that two. And a bitter lemon. And a Perrier, with lots of ice.'

But even more than for the simplicity of glasses of red and white wine, I long for something else. This is for the tea-trays that, in my youth, would be passed down the rows in an interval. Indeed, sometimes, as I drowse at some play by Edward Bond or Howard Barker, I hear a phantasmal clinking of crockery and cutlery and a surreptitious whispering of some aged usherette: 'No, dear, only one choccy biccy on each plate. Use

CRUSH BAR

TO THE
GLORIOUS
DEAD —
FALLEN IN
THE STRUGGLE
FOR DRINKS
IN THE
INTERVAL

'The 'Crush Bar' of the average theatre is all too aptly named.'

the Garibaldis to make up the three.' I rouse myself eagerly, then once again relapse into my previous torpor.

I am always reluctant to complain about the acoustics of our newer theatres, because of my last encounter with Bill Darlington, then septuagenarian theatre critic of the *Daily Telegraph*. We found ourselves next to each other in the stalls of the Theatre Royal in Brighton, where the acoustics are perfect. 'What's the matter with the theatre these days?' he grumbled in the interval. 'Everything has to be played in semi-darkness and the actors have either never learned or have forgotten how to project their voices.' The lighting of the play, a comedy, had been exceptionally bright, and I had missed not a word. Clearly the old boy was going blind and deaf. Perhaps, without my realising it, the same thing is happening to me.

When I once commented on the notoriously bad acoustics of the Olivier to that splendid veteran actor Robert Harris, he replied crisply: 'No excuse for inaudibility. A professional actor should be able to make himself heard *anywhere*.' This was subsequently proved to me in another notoriously difficult auditorium, that at Chichester, when, in *The Aspern Papers*, Cathleen Nesbitt, nonagenarian former girl-friend of Rupert Brooke — not lover, she would always be at pains to insist — could be perfectly heard when a number of her far younger colleagues intermittently could not.

As I wearily tramp down that desolate, windswept tunnel that leads to the Barbican, am beaten in the race to a taxi on Waterloo Bridge by someone half my age after a fatiguing play at the National, fight my way to some overcrowded loo ('I'd always heard that Bath was a fashionable watering-place,' a fellow critic quipped to me in the Theatre Royal there), or am fastidiously ignored by a lady-like barman, I often ask myself why I am not sitting at home beside the fire, with a glass of brandy and a book. Perhaps the directors of our subsidised theatres are right after all. Perhaps I, too, unconsciously subscribe to their belief: it must be good if it's so uncomfortable.

JAZZ

London's jazz scene has always been geographically diverse. In Manhattan one could always take in two or three venues a night, walking, say, from Slugs on the Lower East Side to the Village Gate and then on to Jimmy Ryan's in midtown. Try walking from the Grey Horse at Kingston to the Tramshed at Woolwich!

Nevertheless if you know your way around there is some enjoyable jazz crawling to be done in London. Pride of place has to go to Ronnie Scott's which is still, just as the *Spy* said twenty years ago, the only truly international place in town. Where else could you hear McCoy Tyner, Art Blakey's Jazz Messengers and Lee Konitz in the space of a few weeks? They recently introduced a cheap admission for club members from Monday to Thursday which makes it good value but its reputation and the fact that it's sometimes classified as a night club does mean that you run the risk of drunken loud-mouthed businessmen having a night out. Jazz doesn't seem to interest them. Ronnie himself still presides with magnificent, deadpan panache. No one can insult an audience with so much style. Sometimes he needs to.

One of the most 'serious' clubs around is the Bass Clef in Coronet Street, Hoxten, even though it's a sod to find for those whose natural habitat is west London. Proprietor Peter Ind, a great bass player and lovely guy, has found the right mix – a consistently interesting and varied programme, a nice relaxed atmosphere and a crowd who are there for the music. On Wednesdays watch the galaxy of young English musicians queueing to get on the stand at the jam session at the end of the evening.

The Hundred Club in Oxford Street still plays on though its heyday was in the trad-revival days of the fifties and sixties.

It's tackier now but it still presents some interesting American visitors occasionally. Archie Slepp for instance was there in 1986.

The Pizza Express in Dean Street has an owner with a total dedication to middle-period jazz. The range of music is a bit limited but they, too, have interesting visiting Americans.

Trendy Covent Garden has spawned a number of small jazz venues. Palookavilles and Brahms and Liszt can be personally recommended. Writing as the trombone half of a trombone/guitar duo which has had more wine bar gigs terminated than most people have had hot dinners I can also strongly recommend the Archduke Wine Bar on the South Bank which has a consistent jazz policy and has never ejected this particular trombone/guitar duo. Obviously a discerning proprietor!

Two jazz pubs stand out: the Prince of Orange at Rotherhithe and the Bull's Head at Barnes – the east river and the west river. The Bull's Head's smoky back room is the jazz bar and it's usually crammed. They attract the best of the home-grown modern jazz scene and also visiting Americans. Even the departure of Albert and Don the Door hasn't changed the place a bit. The only slight reservation is the frequency with which certain musicians seem to appear – tonight the Tony Lee trio with Bill Le Sage, tomorrow the Bill Le Sage quartet featuring Tony Lee. Is the Bull's Head in the grip of some booking mafia?

Favourite place of all, maybe not the best but with an ambience all its own, used to be called Davina's. I've known it for twenty years and first played there with Colin James of the Morgan/James duo (who remembers them?!) It belongs to an era when there were atmospheric Soho clubs like the Nucleus, the Spider's Den and Sam Widges and to a time when I was discovering Miles and Charlie Parker. It's a link with the past. It's now called the Six O Six and can be found at the grotty end of the King's Road. It's a members-only club opening at about 11 pm and closing God knows when. Steve Rubie runs it in a most determined uncommercial way. If he doesn't like you, you don't get membership no matter who you are. There's food and wine at very reasonable prices and Steve employs a band, usually a trio, seven nights a week. Steve may very well sit in himself – he plays excellent flute and tenor – and the place is always packed with musicians winding down after their commercial evening gigs. There are plenty of other night people – restaurant workers, taxi drivers, struggling actors. It's down steep steps in a cellar, dimly lit, very smoky, and hardly any room for the rhythm section to set up, huddled round the piano with a faded photo of the late Lenny Felix smiling down sardonically. The drum kit frequently blocks off the entrance to the food store so there may be an extra cymbal accent when Steve or Rene want another tin of something. Nevertheless a surprising variety of good musicians work there for peanuts and when the American big bands are in town you may be lucky and catch one of the sidemen, tie off, sweating like a pig and blowing his heart out.

I make no apologies for this personalised, highly idiosyncratic reflection on the jazz scene in London. Yes, I know, I haven't even mentioned the Town and Country Club, the Atlantic in Brixton or the Plough at Stockwell, but you can always buy *Time Out* for a proper guide. As C. L. R. James might have said, 'What do they know of jazz clubs who only jazz clubs know?'

WALKING

Los Angeles is the greatest non-walking city in the world; Venice its direct opposite. In Beverly Hills the pedestrian, if not actually shot on sight, would certainly get taken in for questioning. In Venice only someone who has never been there thinks that the best way of seeing Venice is by gondola.

London comes somewhere in between. There are no pedestrianised *AltStadts* like the cobbled curiosities of West Germany, but London drivers are not quite so contemptuous of people on feet as the Romans or Parisians. The Burlington Arcade is one of the world's best and oldest shopping precincts; and there are the parks.

For a serious walk, however, the best place is the towpath of the canal or of the Thames. Watch out for flashers, broken glass, dead birds and general decrepitude. Go west.

Every year schools round Isleworth organise a marathon charity walk in aid of a local hospital. The twenty-five-mile round trip has moments of tarmac and tedium, but for the most part it takes you through some of the very best of London's countryside. You'll need stout shoes and thick soles to do the whole trek in a single session, but if you're not feeling too energetic it should be possible to extract a manageable segment.

This is how it goes.

Start in Isleworth opposite the London Apprentice, a famous old pub, which can get overcrowded with sub-yuppies during peak hours. Head northeast along Park Road, skirting the Duke of Northumberland's Syon Park, home of London's largest garden centre. There's a slightly boring bit next up Brentford High Street, but you might pause at the Waterman's Art Centre for a cup of coffee or a drink. They invariably have an interesting art exhibition, and jazz before Sunday lunch.

Press on to Kew Bridge and, staying on the north side of the river, slip down on to the wide tarmac footpath of Strand on the Green. Dinky, over-priced bijou houses, ancient and modern, with little walls protecting front doors from flood; a couple of pubs with drinkers sitting outside on the river walls. At the end of the footpath you edge back into suburban main road, past a modern marina with blocks of smart flats all round, then, leaving the home of Fulham's not very good rugby league club on your left, you pass Chiswick Bridge on your right and enter Duke's Meadows. This is the finishing point for the Oxford and Cambridge Boat Race and a goodish spot for a picnic. There are even one or two picnic tables, though the view of Watney's Brewery leaves more and more to be desired as the firm 'modernises' its plant and on a breezy summer's day it's murder for anyone with hay fever.

At Barnes railway bridge you hang a right and cross the Thames by the footpath alongside the track, then walk south down White Hart Lane with its increasingly chic shops. Pause and examine Kate Dyson's Dining-Room Shop window. Not for nothing is this one of London's endless 'little Chelseas'. Cross the South Circular and carry on up Priory Lane leaving Rosslyn Park Rugby Club on your left and one of London's poshest psychiatric nursing homes on your right, then pass some expensive Tudorbethan stockbrokery and enter Richmond Park by the Roehampton Gate.

Glory be to Richmond Park! The deer! The rhododendrons! The azaleas! The woman who walks her pet otter! The opera singer who practises her arias in Spankers Hill Wood! The badgers! The PR girl from the Dorchester Hotel who rides there every Saturday morning! *Rus in urbe*! We could be in any Capability Brown landscape in the whole of England were it not for the traffic on the orbital road and the people, my dear, the people!

The traipse is west southwest to the Ham Gate where you walk past the elegant and opulent Georgian pile occupied by Lady Annabel Goldsmith before turning left along the Richmond to Kingston road, past British Aerospace and down to the Thames again. In Kingston you switch banks once more following the Barge Walk which sweeps round the park of Hampton Court and up to the Palace.

There is a railway station (Network SouthEast) just over the bridge on the East Molesey side of the river if you are exhausted. On the school charity marathon they provide a pit stop by the side of the Palace where walkers can sit down, massage weary feet, and have a drink. The leisurely pleasure walker may wish to wander off and inspect the great vine or celebrate the arcane glories of real tennis. Once on your way again, you will strike left across the Palace forecourt, past the maze and emerge opposite the entrance to Bushey Park. Like Richmond Park this has deer, but it is flat. Circle the attractive Diana Fountain and continue north up the hurricane-ravaged chestnut avenue before hitting another of the rare boring bits on this walk.

This takes you left along Queens Road to a roundabout where you turn right down Teddington High Street towards the lock. Notice the chi-chi quality of the High Street with its smart restaurants and wine bars – a tribute to the expense-account living of those employed at Thames Television nearby! Before the river you turn north towards Twickenham, a dull patch redeemed only – and then only just – by an extravagant mock-Tudor convent school on the right and an ugly modern pub on the site of Alexander Pope's grotto. There is a pleasant riverside garden opposite.

At Twickenham, cut down to the embankment opposite Eel Pie Island past the parish church and on to the Warren towpath which runs along the edge of the Marble Hill grounds. Marble Hill House is plain, white, simple, beautiful, and a casualty of the demise of the GLC. Great place for a party. On the opposite side you can see the massive Star and Garter Home for disabled servicemen which has the best view in London. Alongside it the Georgian terraces of Richmond. A little further on by Richmond Bridge you can gauge the newest Thameside development – a huge, much-delayed assortment of offices and restaurants, shops and offices by

Quinlan Terry. There are too many offices in Richmond already. Mr Terry's design is thought mimsy and cautious by some; classical by others. At least it removes a decayed blot from the landscape.

You are almost there now. Along Duck's Walk. Up Ranelagh Lane. You will have to cut inland briefly before reaching the Upper Square at Isleworth. Stagger down the last few (pretty) yards to the London Apprentice and if you have timed it right, the bars will be open and you can down a much-needed pint.

This is the best walk in London. If you are reasonably fit, you should be able to start at nine and be finished by opening time at six. That's a strenuous day but not absurd. A reasonably athletic thirteen year old can manage it in rather less!

FLORA

London is not renowned for smiling appreciatively, or even comprehendingly, on its native flowers. When a group of local conservationists tried recently to reintroduce primroses to Primrose Hill, they were smartly rebuffed by the local authority, who said they had quite enough trees already, thank you. London Rocket (which acquired its name and reputation from shooting spectacularly through the rubble after the Great Fire in 1666) was driven out in the nineteenth century. London Pride is now better known as a real ale than an occasional escape from suburban rockeries. The only truly wild species to openly commemorate the capital is a drab hybrid ragwort, *Senecio londinensis*. Its appalling parentage – *S. squalidus* out of *S. viscosus* – sounds like a pedigree from Mayhew's accounts of the London underworld.

But it's a salutary reminder that most urban plants are themselves vagrants, opportunists, troglodytes, making do with whatever little pockets of dereliction they can find. When things are unsettled, and vigilance low, the squatters move in. Or dig in. There are, here and there, a few obstinate relics of the more rustic flora that flourished when London was a collection of villages. Bluebells survive in some of the boskier squares and gardens. There are rabbit-grazed meadows of ox-eye daisy, red campion and buttercups amid the shorn grass of Hyde Park, and seashore plants that the brackish Thames has lapped inland as far as Battersea. There are even orchids on the sacrosanct turf of a south London cemetery (though those in the boggier parts of Hampstead were 'insinuated', by night, by some local enthusiasts anxious to get the Heath some better protection).

Mostly, London's wild flowers are of a more footloose and decidedly metropolitan cast, and they mark out the city's cultural and commercial divisions with uncanny accuracy. From the south and west sweep in the commuters, thrown out of back gardens, hitching in by train or car, a collection of rather respectable European (or at least Atlantic Alliance) plants. From the north and east some stowaways and artisans, plants sprung from the spillage from breweries and food warehouses, a more ephemeral, cosmopolitan crew.

You could draw even more precise social and historical profiles. Naturalised garden plants are one of the great stocks-in-trade of urban flora. The drifts of American golden rod and michaelmas daisy that now line the edges of railway tracks and National Car Parks mostly date from after the war, when their rather gross, spreading luxuriance went out of fashion in utility gardens. The awesome architecture of the giant Caucasian hogweed (it grows ten feet tall and has flower heads the size of car wheels) got it thrown out rather earlier. The best colonies are out towards Brent, but there are good pockets in the damp patches of Regent's Park. It's not a popular species, as contact with its stems can bring sensitive skins out in rashes, but there's no danger of it being wiped out while the great parent colonies, introduced by Queen Victoria, survive in Buckingham Palace Gardens, where skins are thicker.

There are plants that poison you, and plants that cure you, too. The livid purple-veined flowers of henbane, one of Dr Crippen's armoury, have cropped up in the car park of the Festival Hall. Deadly nightshade grew till quite recently in the grounds of Guy's Hospital, where it may once have been cultivated as a sedative. Dormant seeds from old herb gardens were probably also the source of the flush of thornapples (like herbaceous conkers) that sprung up in gardens throughout London during the heatwave of 1975. But why precisely, the yellow pea-flowers and inflated seed cases of bladder senna (once grown as a cheap laxative) should be so conspicuous in railway sidings just north and east of Liverpool Street is a secret known only to British Rail and the City.

Food plants are usually much more explicable, and certainly

vastly more widespread. Tomato plants grow on just about every waste patch and rubbish tip. So do the commoner spices and herbs — fennel, dill, coriander — anywhere that seeds might be spilt from a jar. More exotic plants like cumin, gram, and water melon have all increased as London's ethnic population has grown, but they tend to be confined to the East-End municipal tips, which have a climate all of their own as well as the accumulated debris of half the capital. But how did the peanut bush which grew near Shepperton, or the giant fig tree that still flourishes in the Ludgate Hill car park, manage to sprout from lunch-pack throwouts and survive in our climate?

London botanising doesn't have to be hedged about with constant ecological and historical paradoxes. There are great spectacles, too. The rose-bay willow herb that once covered London in the aftermath of the Blitz has declined, but buddleia bushes (introduced about 1890) have turned the rubble of abandoned shunting yards and demolition sites into passable imitations of Chinese foothills. And a walk along the canals through Islington is now a wonderfully incongruous trip, with ancient waterside flowers — gipsywort, skullcap, balsams — flowering in the most refined pastel shades against a riotous backdrop of technicolour graffiti.

Yet what is really most intriguing about London flora is not so much *what* turns up as the where and how of it. The whole company makes up an extraordinary saga of opportunism and adaptation. The Victorians would have loved it as a parable of survival in the most frugal circumstances. So would Alexander Pope, given that there it is, in the most literal sense, 'where'er you walk'.

Bright blue lobelias in the pavement cracks seeded from a second floor window box. Ferns in the basement, revelling in the shade. (In Belgrave Square I've seen one straining against the glass insert of a manhole cover.) Bird-seed species, like canary grass, sprouting in minimal soils at the foot of street trees. And one ubiquitous species, in doorstep tubs, at the foot of hoardings, even growing from the now less frequently swept gutters, that Londoners have made some gesture towards adopting. *Galinsoga parviflora* is, rather fittingly, an unprepossessing daisy from the Third World, Peru to be precise. It was first noticed in Richmond in the 1890s, where it had presumably escaped from Kew Gardens, and became known locally as Kew-weed. Then its seeds began wafting over less elegant postal districts, and a more down-to-earth and popular name was needed. *Galinsoga parviflora* was too much of a mouthful for most Londoners, so with the nicest sense of irony it was bowdlerised into Gallant Soldiers.

SAILING

The most important part of sailing is not participating in it, but talking about it. It's the talking, rather than the participating, that matters. That is why most sailing clubs offer generous facilities for talking (often at the expense of those for changing) with, more often than not, a bar to encourage the flow of conversation, reminiscing, point-making and general exaggeration that seems natural to devotees.

Although London is some distance from the sea, it is well served by sailing clubs. The governing body of the sport, the Royal Yachting Association, lists some 143 in their Thames Valley Area. These can be divided into two distinct groups – those clubs whose members can sail on adjacent waters, and those clubs who can only offer talking facilities – their sailing being conducted on distant waters away from London.

Of the latter the senior must be the Royal Thames Yacht Club whose antecedents go back to the very beginnings of yachting. It all began on the Thames. Charles II on his restoration, was presented with a pleasure boat or *jaght* by the Dutch. Named *Mary*, it arrived in the Thames in 1660. In the following year local builders completed some copies, enabling the first race, from Greenwich to Gravesend and back, to take place for a wager of £100. The King's craft was accompanied by his barge and a kitchen boat and yachting, it would appear, remained the sport of kings for the next hundred years or so, for it was not until 1775 that the Duke of Cumberland presented a silver cup for sailing vessels 'never let out for hire' for a race from Westminster Bridge to Putney and back.

As a result of this race, the Cumberland Fleet was formed and on the coronation of George IV it was renamed, somewhat obsequiously, the 'Coronation Society'. After an internal

dispute (yacht racing has always been a serious matter and in early days it was not unknown for rival craft to attack each others' rigging with swords) the Coronation Society split, with a breakaway group forming the Thames Yacht Club which in 1830 became the Royal Thames. Although its sailing activities have moved away, it has retained a London club-house. Local sailing, however, is now confined to the very occasional, none too serious race on the Serpentine, its main interest is in in-shore racing and trying to win back the America's Cup.

Of more recent origin is the Royal Ocean Racing Club, the home of ocean racing and governing body of the sport. It was founded after the first European ocean race in 1925, which took place from the Isle of Wight to the Fastnet Rock off Southern Island and back to Plymouth. Would-be members must have completed a Fastnet race or 400 miles off-shore including two nights at sea. The Royal Ocean Racing Club certainly insists that members must have done it before they can talk about it.

A third London club, and the junior of the three, is the Little Ship Club in the City of London. Founded in 1926, it resulted from a letter in a yachting journal by Maurice Griffith suggesting it would be useful to have a club where members could chat about sailing. The club takes a pretty relaxed view of sailing, and is more interested in cruising. Would-be members need not have sailed but should have a general interest in the subject.

There are also a number of clubs in the London area representing larger organisations ranging from the City Livery, the Bar, Lloyds, London School of Economics, Polsky, and what could well become a collector's item, the GLC Yacht Cruising Club.

The clubs that actually offer their members on-the-spot sailing, come in several distinct groups. The oldest are the river clubs along the Thames, starting with Ranelagh at Putney. Most of the clubs are of Victorian origin, the club-houses, despite a touch of formica, appear to be still haunted by bewhiskered sailors taking a break from saving or building the Empire.

After the Ranelagh we come to the London Corinthian of A.P. Herbert fame, now in a splendid Georgian clubhouse; Tamesis; Thames United; Minina; Thames Sailing Club, the oldest of the non-tidal clubs; Laleham, and queen of them all; the Upper Thames at Bourne End. Bourne End week was once as much part of the social calendar as Ascot, Henley and Cowes. All these clubs started with a motley rag-bag of craft, sailing to complicated handicaps, which were replaced over the years by more closely controlled classes to allow boat for boat racing. River sailors tend to be somewhat intense, having to be adept at making the most of the varying currents and winds that can shift abruptly in both force and direction.

In the 1920s and 30s sailors moved to some of the smaller canal reservoirs round London: the Welsh Harp, Ruislip, Aldenham, and the occasional gravel pit, Rickmansworth being typical. These small reservoir sailors tend to be known as 'pondies' by people who sail on the sea or the river.

In the 1960s, dinghy sailing as a sport exploded and every conceivable stretch of water was pressed into service with new clubs springing up in simple prefab, lookalike clubhouses. Any area where there is any water is pretty certain to have a club, even if some of them are finding the odd motorway being driven through their water.

Finally, in the 1970s, the mega London clubs came into being with the RYA persuading Thames Water that there was no danger from pollution if they allowed yachtsmen to sail on the massive reservoirs that surround London. These clubs go back to the royal origin of sailing, because the old water authority named its reservoirs after the kings and queens. Thus there are clubs like King George V, Queen Mary and most recently, Queen Mother, which to avoid confusion, named itself Datchet Sailing Club. Hard by Windsor Castle, 3½ miles around, it offers superb sailing with fleets of thirty or more keelboats, dinghies, catamarans and the ubiquitous sailboards which are now coming to the rescue of so many clubs whose treasurers are hard-pressed to balance the books.

Sailing in London used to be carried out by professionals for owners who preferred to watch from the shore or at least sit in comfort on the deck leaving others to do the work. Lord Cardigan of *Charge of the Light Brigade* fame, is alleged to have remarked when asked if he would care to take the helm of his craft, 'I take nothing between meals.'

Nowadays Lord Cardigan would be asked – politely – to find another sailing club.

RIDING IN HYDE PARK

Between the traffic ferment of Hyde Park Corner and the ornamental phallus of the Albert Memorial, on the south side of Hyde Park, stretches Rotten Row; its name apparently an anglicised form of Route du Roi.

Along the sand and gravelled length, beneath the tall, gaunt, winter trees, dripping distantly, the riders pass, circling round the bowling greens and returning by the south carriageway, or turning towards Marble Arch and the northern circuit. Cavalry officers from Knightsbridge Barracks dutifully exercising large black horses, members of the BBC and Civil Service riding clubs; zealous in their cultivation of what can never be more than mediocre skills; cold, crash-capped children, shivering inside their anoraks as they trot by on bored ponies; and an orderly group from the local riding school, sweatered and huskied, tentatively steering their solid, sober, well-trimmed mounts. The horsemen rarely raise a glance from their fellow park users, the hunched bicyclists, the popinjay joggers, and preoccupied dog walkers.

'It being a foul day, and cold there are few go to the park . . .' Pepys had written in the days when, seeking preferment, a ride in the Row might enable you to catch the eye of Charles II. It was Henry VIII who, coveting the 600 acres of wild country so conveniently close to London, compelled the Abbot of Westminster Abbey to exchange it for a much less desirable parcel of land in Berkshire, but selfishly, he fenced the park to make a private hunting ground; and it was not until the Stuarts came to the throne that Hyde Park was opened to the public.

The Row and the Ring quickly became places where the fashionable went, 'To see and be seen or to learn the gossip of the hour.' It was not always an enjoyable experience as

Pepys' visit in a friend's coach shows: 'Thence to the park, where no pleasure – there being too much dust. Little company. And one of the horses almost spoiled by falling down and getting his legs over the pole. But all mended presently.'

Later he reports 1,000 coaches taking their occupants to watch a muster of the Guards and, in 1668, when he has bought his own coach, 'And thence to the Park ... where with mighty pride rode up and down ... and I thought our horses and coach as pretty as any there, and observed to be so by others.'

A year later the pleasures of ownership had not waned, but he had begun to complain about the number of hackney coaches in the Park, which obscured the more elegant private turnouts.

In the 1690s, with William III living at the newly built Kensington Palace, government ministers and other visitors crossing the park were constantly attacked by footpads and thieves so the King had 300 oil lamps erected and made London's first lighted highway.

Queen Anne took an extra thirty acres of the park into the palace gardens and built the orangery, but it was George II's Queen Caroline who conceived the idea of the Serpentine which, with Long Water and the Round Pond, was man-made, but fed by the Westbourne stream.

While Kensington Gardens was closed to the public (until Queen Victoria opened it to all those who were respectably dressed) Hyde Park was shared with the people. The Prince Regent rode there with the Tsar of Russia and the King of Prussia during their state visit in 1814. In August of the same year, the season over, he gave orders that peace was to be celebrated and Wellington honoured by extravagant junketings. A naval battle was re-enacted on the Serpentine, there were balloon ascents, and oriental temples, pagodas, and booths were everywhere. *The Times* was disapproving and, on 9 August 1814, Charles Lamb wrote to Wordsworth. 'The very colour of green is vanished. The whole of Hyde Park is dry, crumbling sand – booths and drinking places go all round it for a mile and a half . . . the stench of liquors, *bad* tobacco, dirty people and provisions, conquers the air . . .' But he did smoke, 'One delicious pipe in one of the cleanliest and goodliest of the booths.' And he enjoyed the splendid fire-works.

Later, Elizabeth Grant, a Highland lady on a visit, was even less enthusiastic about the fashionable entertainment offered by the Row. 'One long file of carriages at a foot's pace going one way, passing another long file of carriages at a foot's pace going the other, bows gravely exchanged between the occupants, when any of the busy starers were acquainted.'

A Victorian publication, *The Book of the Horse*, is very severe on people who, at the height of the season, ride horses in the Row 'which are as much out of place as a coalheaver in the costume of his trade in the stalls of the opera. The park hack of every man or woman who aspires to fashionable distinction, or has become a public character, should be handsome if ridden by the young, and have "character" if the rider be neither young nor of a good horseback figure. The head must be of the finest oriental type, the neck well arched . . . The mane and tail should be full, straight, without the least suspicion of a curl, and every hair as soft as silk. Perfect symmetry with perfect temper, luxurious paces and perfect manners as regards his rider and other horses. A park hack is essentially an ornamental animal.'

But for the early morning riders, out for exercise, standards were less demanding: 'One Chief Justice prefers a Leicester-shire hunter, another learned brother a fat pony . . . a Queen's counsel seems to have a fancy for the cast-off weeds of a racing stable. The young Greek merchant is always seen on one valued at three good figures and when Greek joins Greek to the tune of half a dozen they will step along – a wonderful sight – with nearly 2,000 pounds of horse flesh in line.'

Lord Melbourne often rode in the park, always on 'a powerful easy paced horse', but Sir Robert Peel was 'an awkward rider'. He refused to buy a perfect hack called

Premier on the grounds that no one paid £400 for a hack, but his cheaper purchase shied on Constitution Hill and Peel was killed by the fall.

An unknown writer gives a sentimental picture:

Of all the sights of London in the month of June there are few prettier than Rotten Row at the hour in the morning when grave merchants of mighty name in the city and the hardworked of Her Majesty's Cabinet and her Majesty's Opposition begin to ride away to their daily, never-ending duties; while the park is alive with little mobs of boys and girls galloping, trotting, and walking as little as possible, with Papa, Mamma, or sister Anne, or mostly with some stout and faithful Ruggles, panting and toiling after his precious charges.

But all this activity vanished with the end of the season and Earl Russell, parodying Goldsmith, wrote:

> Remote, unfriended, melancholy, slow,
> A single horseman faces Rotten Row;
> In Brooks's sits one quidnunc, to peruse
> The broad dull sheet which tells the lack of news
> At White's a lonely Brummel lifts his glass
> To see two empty hackney coaches pass.

Until the IRA bomb in 1983, the Household Cavalry used to exercise regularly and *en masse* in the Park, but now their routes and times are deliberately unpredictable. The old custom of allowing accomplished civilian riders to exercise the Cavalry horses has also been discontinued and anyone who really wants a ride down Rotten Row would be best advised to contact Lilo Blum's, the best known riding school in London.

AFTERWORDS

THE WORST

You still see them. See whom? The poor. Oh, must we go into that? Just a paragraph or two. Worth skipping? If you must. You still see them, wrapped in newspapers and packaged in cardboard, on the ventilating grilles above the kitchen of the grand hotels, under the railway arches at Waterloo, wherever easement from the elements may be found. But the scale of the misery, although an outrage in a welfare state, is modest compared to the London of Blake and de Quincey, of Mayhew and Dickens, of Arthur Morrison and George Orwell. Here is a description of the squalor of Whitechapel in 1827:

The putrid mixture of gore and excrementitious matters proceeding from the animals slaughtered there, instead of passing into the common sewer, is daily disposed over the whole surface of that wide street, in place of pure water, which in all other parts of the metropolis is used! The putrefying miasmata exhaled from this under the influence of a scorching sun, and wafted down the close and narrow lanes by the sultry breezes of summer, is, and must be, a most productive cause of typhus fever, and other putrid diseases as they are termed, which at this season abound in that neighbourhood. Were human ingenuity taxed to compound a malaria of concentrated power, none more deadly could be imagined.

Through such streets roamed the 'pure' (dung) collectors, who took their pailfuls to the tanneries, the rat-catchers and bug-disposers, the sewer-hunters and the cat's meat men. (Pussy meat was eaten on a skewer without salt.)

By comparison then, contemporary London is strangely civilised and curiously bland. One of the great train robbers sells flowers anonymously outside Waterloo station. The cells administered by the Brentford police are centrally heated and air-conditioned. The old dock buildings, once haunts of Cypriot ponces and oriental hashish-sellers, have been converted into state-of-the-art homes for publishers and ad-men. They play Hawaiian guitar music at you as you squat over the automatic lavatory in Leicester Square (and elsewhere I expect, although I will not carry my researches to ludicrous extremes) and the horrors exhibited in the London Dungeons or the Chamber of Horrors at Madame Tussaud's are pale simulacra of murderers and monsters of the past.

Well, actually no. I must contradict myself. The horrors of the London Dungeons are not pale but blood-bespattered; here are dissections, disembowellings, impalings, amputations and tortures recreated in gloating detail and awarded a Special Commendation by the London Tourist Board.

Real horrors there are, of course, but fewer than you might suppose. Guess how many muggings occur daily on the London Underground? Five, ten, twenty, one hundred? According to the Ministry of Transport, two. And only one in four are women. Nonetheless you might wish to avoid Victoria (worst for pickpockets and indecent assaults), Oxford Circus (worst for robberies) and King's Cross (worst for muggings). Comparisons with the past are again reassur-ing. Highwaymen, cutpurses and revolutionaries abounded, and gangs of eighteenth-century yuppies, known as 'Mohocks', removed the ears of pedestrians who caught their fancy. Public executions were on a cataclysmic scale with 50,000 people being hanged at Tyburn, of whom eighty-one were martyrs. A cautious subway user of today is probably safer than an old-fashioned heretic, at least in this life; but then heresies are not what they used to be, not since they were made respectable by the Bishop of Durham.

If you are not to freeze to death, nor to inhale the 'putrefying miasmata', nor to starve, nor to be mugged, nor to be hanged, and if you can avoid the consequences of drugs and meths and Aids, what *is* the worst that can overtake you?

You might be clamped. And that is bad. The cost is not as steep as the cost of being towed away, but it is just as humiliating. If clamped in the West End, you are required to

present yourself in the underground car park at Marble Arch. You follow dank, graffiti-lined tunnels, reminiscent of *Indiana Jones and the Temple of Doom* to – how to characterise it? – to a sort of Kafkaesque hell-hole in which docile queues of sheepish shoppers stand in line, awaiting the dead fish-eyes of bureaucratic androids to whom money must be passed.

'We advise you to wait by your car,' they intone, and it is impossible to see their lips move.

'For how long?'

'The average is between four and six hours at present.'

'But the temperature is seven below, and it's Christmas Eve . . .'

And then they smile, a seedy smile revealing tobacco-stained teeth from between which escapes the stale odour of decayed dreams.

And the system is so inefficient . . .

You might very likely be rooked. In so many ways. By the ice-cream vendors at the tourist hot-spots (avoid, incidentally, the Tower of London. There's little to see but the Crown Jewels, and it takes you a reign or two before you're admitted. And it's not even as if the Princes were actually murdered in the Bloody Tower). By the West End theatres which charge as much for seat DI at £18.50, plus agents' fees, as for C20, and then require you to pay a pound for a promotional programme, which ought of course to be free. By the publicans who try to stop you eating your food in their pubs, no matter how much you spend on their beer. By the cowboy auctioneers, who take out full page and misleading advertisements in the *Evening Standard* and then take you for the hammer price, plus the premium, plus VAT on both, with bids off the walls and all the trimmings; and by the smart auctioneers whose Machiavellian subtleties are more sophisticated. (I sold goods at Lots Road Galleries for a total of over £200 and received a cheque for a little over £60, after deductions for 'minimum commission', insurance, storage, and Bob's your uncle.) By the chocolate machines in the stations which promise the fainting traveller fruit and nut,

'You might very likely be rooked . . .
by the chocolate machines.'

and deliver nothing. The District Line (westward) at South Kensington is notorious, but *Which* reports that one out of four attempts to get chocolate from any machine ends in failure, and one out of eight attempts in the loss of your money. Or the garagemen who . . . Or the stationmaster who . . . Or the doctor who . . . But, enough. I begin to sound like the club bore.

All I really mean to add is that the worst sights in London are the small, unidentifiable animals on spits in the windows of Chinatown restaurants, and the sad eyes of horses up for sale (and then what?) at the Southall Horse Fair, and the drooping tails of the puppies in Club Row.

And the worst sounds are the whooping chortles of Hooray Henries in wine bars, and the snap and crunch of an underfoot cockroach in a King's Cross curry house.

And the worst smells are from the monkey house at the zoo, because the smell of captivity is always rancid, and from the lifts of multi-storey car parks.

And the most boring monument is Cleopatra's Needle.

THE FUTURE

A window over Docklands is a good point from which to predict the nature of London which will be reviewed by the next generation of spies. Cranes swoop, pneumatic drills drill, concrete mixers mix. The sliver of river still left by the developers is empty but not for long . . .

A man returning from service in the 'John Company', the Honourable East India Company which became India in 1703, the year Ned Ward's Discreet Guide to the Pleasures of the Capital appeared, would have found it quicker to walk to Southwark from Deptford than go upstream by boat, so dense was the traffic. It will return. London is returning to its source, the Thames, the great river which made it the biggest and the richest city in the world for 200 years.

By 2003 AD or After the Common Era as it might be called, Christianity having been abandoned as the state religion, the Thames will be dammed and restored as a navigable thoroughfare. The grandest and fanciest emporia and dwellings, of which the Galleria in Hay's Wharf is recognised as the pioneer, crowd its banks. At first city gents – a decreasing number of gentlemen – take to the river in miniature hovercrafts called 'mudlarks', but these are banned for their noise and replaced by tiny and elegant steam yachts powered by coal, deemed more ecologically sound than diesel or petrol.

Domestic service, having returned as an acceptable and profitable metier, the yachts are manned by crews clad in the livery of commodity brokers and investment bankers who supply them to their executives in lieu of the Porsches of today, samples of which can be seen in transport museums. Twenty-first century 'Yuppies', some of them quite old, use airships for provincial journeys and can rocket to Brazil for the weekend. London is a zone of silence. The Underground system remains, but the noise of transport in the arcades of Piccadilly and Oxford Street is reduced to the sound of shuffling feet, and the hum of moving pavements for the lazy.

The millennia balls of 2000, each on a historical theme, were so successful that some people never take off their costumes, so that in Waterlow Park bewigged gentlemen and their courtesans people the supermarkets to the dismay of shopping-mall detectives, who consider their elaborate rig only too suitable for 'hoisting'. Little Venice went, predictably, Venetian. Even the delivery boys – oh yes they, too, have been restored – are masked and the warm nights throb with amateur arias.

The nights are always warm from the cloud-piercing domes which cover much of central London. One can always wrap up and go out into the parks if nostalgic for mist and drizzle.

The millennia celebrations in Notting Hill Gate, with the Zulu warrior Tchaka as its theme, degenerates into a battle between rival impis, but the police posted on the rooftops with their crossbows wisely withholding fire, allow the combatants to slaughter each other amiably. (In reaction to the Hungerford Massacre of the late eighties – or was it the early nineties? – firearms are no longer used in the UK.)

Notting Hill Gate has become tribal, a sort of Delphi of the black world, and hundreds of thousands of black pilgrims report annually to their imagined chiefs to the delight of the London Tourist Board, the second most influential body in the city.

Another tourist attraction is the Forum Philippi, so called after Philip Howard, Literary Editor of *The Times*, now merged with the *Financial Times*, whose advocacy of a reconstructed Roman city on the site of the Mint, was successful and realised by Sir Roy Strong in his old age. The slave market is re-enacted on the Thursday of the Easter weekend, but slaves can reject bids if they don't like the look of the purchasers. The juvenile section is especially popular: recruited from casts of the play *Androcles and the Lion* which is still a favourite in enough secondary schools. The children return contented to their parents, with armfuls of presents after the holiday, more or less intact.

The realisation of fantasies is the official policy of the new City of London Authority (known as CLAUT), and is ordered on a local, almost village, basis, allowing controlled indulgence in every conceivable human drive and conception. You can ski in real snow on Primrose Hill, bet on cocks fighting near the Globe in Southwark, get seriously hurt in a joust on Blackheath. The nudist colony by Lots Road Power Station – now the biggest sauna in the world – has heated and sanded its section of the Thames but often has to repel young people clad in bathing suits from its beaches.

Sex shops, sex shows have vanished and indeed sex crimes are almost unknown, largely, it is thought, as a side effect of the fantasy boom which has stripped discretion from London's pleasures, and made them available internationally.

Orwell's prophesies are unfulfilled but animal farms are everywhere. Every school has one and many families have a cow bred back, by the CLAUT experimental farm in the gardens of Buckingham's Palace, to an animal the size of a dalmatian, best milked by children – a triumph for the slogan 'three square metres and a cow'!

London was nearly swamped by its aging population at the turn of the millennium but the Euthanasia Centre in the reconstituted Crystal Palace has proved a tactful and charming venue for the departing of all classes. At the other end of the human scale, child abuse is a thing of the past since work was severely rationed for the parents of young children. Drugs of all kinds including nicotine can be had on prescription but their use has diminished with the decrease of boredom and stress due to the variety and licence of available activities. The universal warmth has generated street life, street concern and street pride. National Service – in the police, post office, hospitals, sanitation or whatever – is compulsory and all wear the same kind of uniform. Senior officers in all branches of the 'Service' are elected. The Civil Liberty Trust in Tabard Street, SE1 (now a shrine for the martyrs of the Bermondsey

Market riots of 1999 in protest at the abolition of money-specia-cash — the last time the police used teargas in London) has recently been successful in lobbying through legislation denying government automatic access to the 'com-deck', the personal video radio communications centre, the size of a wristwatch, which is issued to every adult. This can now be switched off and the right to be incommunicado is protected by international law.

If this picture of London in the twenty-first century is thought unlikely by those of a dystopic inclination, remember it is the responsibility of the prophet to say not what will happen but what should.